VINTAGE ST. PETE

The golden age of tourism – and more

Published by St. Petersburg Press

St. Petersburg, FL

www.stpetersburgpress.com

Copyright ©2020

All rights reserved. No part of this publication may be reproduced, distributed, or transmitted in any form or by any means, including photocopying, recording or other electronic or mechanical methods, without the prior written permission of the publisher, except in the case of brief quotations embodied in critical reviews and certain other noncommercial uses permitted by copyright law. For permission requests contact St. Petersburg Press at www.stpetersburgpress.com.

Design and composition by St. Petersburg Press

Cover and interior design by St. Petersburg Press and Pablo Guidi

Hardcover ISBN: 978-1-940300-22-1

Paperback ISBN: 978-1-940300-23-8

First Edition

VINTAGE ST. PETE

The golden age of tourism – and more

Bill DeYoung

©2020 St. Petersburg Press
All stories previously published in the *St. Pete Catalyst* 2018-2020

Table of Contents

Foreword 3

TOURIST ATTRACTIONS

Sunken Gardens 6
Webb's City 13
Marine Arena 24
Tiki Gardens 32
The London Wax Museum 42
The Aquatarium 52
MGM's Bounty 59

HISTORY

The Pier 70
Capone, the Babe and Jungle Prada 78
Earl Gresh Wood Parade 84
Fort De Soto 92
Marilyn Monroe & Joe DiMaggio 99
Boyd Hill Nature Trail 105
Suncoast Seabird Sanctuary 114

ENTERTAINMENT & FUN

Manhattan Casino 124
The Operetta and the Music Circus 137
Bayfront Center 148
Gay Blades Roller Rink 155
Dr. Paul Bearer 163

THE MOVIES

Sun Haven Studios 170
HEALTH 178
COCOON 184

VINTAGE ST. PETE

The golden age of tourism – and more

Bill DeYoung

©2020 St. Petersburg Press
All stories previously published in the *St. Pete Catalyst* 2018-2020

Table of Contents

Foreword 3

TOURIST ATTRACTIONS

Sunken Gardens 6
Webb's City 13
Marine Arena 24
Tiki Gardens 32
The London Wax Museum 42
The Aquatarium 52
MGM's Bounty 59

HISTORY

The Pier 70
Capone, the Babe and Jungle Prada 78
Earl Gresh Wood Parade 84
Fort De Soto 92
Marilyn Monroe & Joe DiMaggio 99
Boyd Hill Nature Trail 105
Suncoast Seabird Sanctuary 114

ENTERTAINMENT & FUN

Manhattan Casino 124
The Operetta and the Music Circus 137
Bayfront Center 148
Gay Blades Roller Rink 155
Dr. Paul Bearer 163

THE MOVIES

Sun Haven Studios 170
HEALTH 178
COCOON 184

Foreword

The City of St. Petersburg, Florida has recently enjoyed a remarkable renaissance of rediscovery.

This quaint little 'burg has quite the buzz today – young and old have found their way back here and you'll find most conversations start with or end with – "I love St Pete." It's just part of how we feel about this place.

There's a feeling of belonging here. Of community. It's not just a tourist destination. It's our home.

We've been Florida's Sunshine City for over 100 years – and we've worked hard to ensure visitors from around the world come here to enjoy our beautiful beaches, amazing climate and natural attractions.

It's his hometown too, so the author takes a prideful romp through some of the quirkiest, carefree and fun-loving experiences of our boomer childhood. He gently reminds us that history has occurred too in our lifetime, and brings to light the personal stories of those who brought us all those postcard memories.

It's a point of pride for me, too, as I know what this book will inspire …

You see, we know our city will continue to attract visitors from around the world. Our home with its world class museums, artists and scientists, breweries, bikes and pets on every corner surrounded on three sides by the most divine coastline will always be attractive for consumers. But what we really seek and call out for are the creators. Those courageous creators willing to share their dreams, their ideas and their lives to bring the next most amazing idea here for all of us to enjoy.

I can't wait to see who's next.

Chris Steinocher
President & CEO
St Petersburg Area Chamber of Commerce

TOURIST ATTRACTIONS

SUNKEN GARDENS

For more than 30 years, Sunken Gardens was one of the Top Ten highest-grossing tourist attractions in Florida. Postcard image.

St. Petersburg might be a very different place today if Titan Marketing Group had purchased Sunken Gardens back in 1999, as the Homosassa-based real estate company planned.

The city's beloved 4.5-acre botanical garden, which had been designated a Historic Site just the year before, was to be transformed into a nudist resort, called Gardens of Eden.

After more than six decades of operation, attendance was at an all-time low, and Sunken Gardens was hemorrhaging money.

"The only thing that can save Sunken Gardens at this point is a niche market," the company's Galen Ballard told the *Orlando Sentinel*. Nudism, he said, "is ideal because these are people looking for privacy and a place to go. The beauty of Sunken Gardens is those 14-foot-high walls, bougainvillea dripping over the walls. You've got total seclusion."

No nudes is good nudes, however, and once the Titan deal collapsed the City of St. Petersburg – under gentle pressure from a committed group of volunteers and Old Northeast neighbors – purchased Sunken Gardens, and has been operating it for 20 years now.

"The City is very happy that we are able to sustain ourselves," says Jennifer Tyson, education and volunteer coordinator. "In the last several years we've actually increased our attendance every single year. So we're doing very well. I think the City absolutely considers it a gem of St. Petersburg, and it's always behind our efforts to preserve the history, and continue to bring Sunken Gardens into the modern era as well."

> *Taking full advantage of St. Petersburg's balmy tropical weather, Turner began by planting banana and papaya trees.*

Attendance at Sunken Gardens averaged around 200,000 in 2018 and 2019.

Maybe it's locals, hungry for no-hurry nostalgia; perhaps it's horticulture enthusiasts, eager to ogle

There are approximately 50,000 tropical plants on the 4.5 acre site, including more than 500 species. Postcard image.

the approximately 50,000 tropical plants on site, including more than 500 species, and marvel at the winding, below-street-level landscaping and lush rainforest canopies.

Then again, there's likely lots of people who don't give a flip about roller coasters, thrill rides, animatronics, 3D and long, long wait times in the blistering summer sun.

One hundred seventeen years have passed since George Turner, a Duval County farm boy, arrived in newly-incorporated St. Petersburg in search of opportunity.

For Turner, this meant a burgeoning city where land was cheap, and where his services as a plumbing contractor would be in demand.

Among the properties he bought in 1911 was a scrubby five-acre lot on Northeast 4th Street. Here, he built the home where he and his new bride Eula would raise their four children. The majority of the land behind the house was consumed by a shallow lake gurgling inside an ancient sinkhole – and Turner, whose hobby was horticulture, devised a way to drain the remaining water, leaving a fertile loam as much as 15 feet deep.

Taking full advantage of St. Petersburg's balmy tropical weather, Turner began by planting banana and papaya trees. But years of winter frosts and Gulf of Mexico thunderstorms made it impractical to operate a self-sustaining, profitable fruit farm. The family produced enough to sell fruit and juice from a hand-made roadside cabin, but George continued to fit pipes and run water lines fulltime for his adopted city.

The garden, however, remained his passion. Over the years, Turner added trees and plants from across Florida, and from around the world, developing winding tiled pathways through the exotic flora, and creating unique waterscapes to accent his dreamy landscaping.

By the 1930s, it had become a Sunday tradition for locals to wander over to the immaculately manicured Turner gardens, for peaceful afternoon strolling. Turner fenced off his property and began charging a nickel admission.

This was increased to 15 cents in 1935, which is when George Turner quit the plumbing business and devoted himself to the development, care and maintenance of what he proudly named "Turner's Sunken Gardens."

Winter visitors here like to car-

George Turner's original 1930s entrance. Postcard image.

ry back Turner memories of Florida's rarer plants, traditional and lush. Towering palms and rich-foliaged banana trees, with bananas in bloom frame the less imposing plants. Roses, petunias, gladioluses, japonicas, royal poincianas, plumbago, hibiscus ramble about the gardens, appear in nooks and crannies by the rock springs and pools. Hundreds of papaya trees bear fruit and the juice is sold for the "pause that refreshes" at a little log house.

St. Petersburg Times, Dec. 19, 1937

In a city where the main attractions were year-round warmth and sunshine, Sunken Gardens became, if not a destination, sort of a cherry on top; if you were visiting St. Petersburg, you went to the beach (were you so inclined), you visited Webb's City and you strolled through Sunken Gardens. Maybe you sat on a green bench.

Turner threw open his gates at almost exactly the same time entrepreneur Dick Pope cut the ribbon on Cypress Gardens, another botanical wonderland, near Winter Haven. Whereas that location backed up to an enormous, deepwater lake and

New York Yankees catcher Yogi Berra and friend, early '60s. City of St. Petersburg.

featured water-ski shows (particularly big in the 1940s and '50s), Sunken Gardens was merely a well-appointed garden, with caged parrots and other tropical birds squawking away between the tree stands.

For tourists of the time, that was enough. Florida itself was what they were coming to experience, and for more than 30 years, Sunken Gardens was one of the Top Ten highest-grossing tourist attractions in the state.

In 1959, a small botanical garden was opened on the grounds of the Anheuser-Busch brewery in Tampa. Although Busch Gardens started expanding in the mid '60s, in the beginning it was nothing more than the "hospitality area" for guests taking beer-making tours.

George Turner died in 1961; sons George Jr. and Ralph took over full-time operations at Sunken Gardens.

In 1964 and '65, Walt Disney began buying up acres of upland and swamp in Central Florida, using an alias so sellers wouldn't artificially jack up their prices. This would be the beginning of the end for hundreds of Florida "roadside attractions," although nobody knew it at the time.

> **The City of St. Petersburg purchased Sunken Gardens for $3.8 million in 1999.**

The junior Turners plowed ahead, spending $175,000 for a vintage Mediterranean-style building adjacent to their property (built in 1926 as the Sanitary Public Market, it had later been home to the American Legion Armory; in '66, when the family bought it, it was a Coca-Cola bottling plant). This became office space and "The World's Largest Gift Shop."

Adjacent to the gift shop, beginning in 1968, was an exhibit called King of Kings, a series of costumed wax figures depicting the life of Christ.

(In 2002, the vintage building was added to the National Register of Historic Places.)

Sunken Gardens survived, and even thrived, during the "golden age" of Bay Area tourist attractions. The numbers, however, don't lie. By the 1980s, attendance was falling way, way off.

Sunken Gardens went on the market in 1989. It remained open, doing decent if not spectacular business, maintained as always by various members of the Turner family, a dedicated staff and an army of volunteers who dearly loved the place. Residents of Old Northeast rallied around the notion of saving Sunken Gardens.

Around the time of the nudist resort fiasco, "They really sensed that Sunken Gardens could be lost," Tyson relates. "It had been 10 years, there were many different failed contracts on it, and so eventually the public, along with some long-term Sunken Gardens employees, really tried to get the community involved.

"Thinking that with community involvement the City might be more likely to purchase the gardens."

St. Petersburg bought Sunken Gardens from three Turner grandsons, for $3.8 million, in 1999. "It was really a community grassroots effort to save the gardens," Tyson says with pride.

WEBB'S CITY

Webb's City (seen here in its '60s heyday) was at the corner of 9th Street and 2nd Avenue South. Postcard image.

From the corner of Rui Farias' office, Doc Webb is always watching.

Farias, director of the St. Petersburg Museum of History, considers Webb – the founder, president, chairman and namesake of Webb's City, the massive retail center that dominated downtown for over half a century – a pivotal figure in local history.

The black and white cardboard standup that leans ever-present in the corner is just shy of life-sized. Webb was a wiry 5-foot-5, weighing 130 pounds, always immaculate in a white linen suit and shined-up white shoes.

He built and ruled an empire that came to cover 10 city blocks. Between the four-story main building on 9th Street and 2nd Avenue South, and the ancillary shops, Webb's City at its zenith included 77 different departments.

It was, at least until the advent of the neighborhood shopping center in the late 1950s, and the suburban mall tsunami of the '70s, the center of the St. Petersburg retail universe.

Webb's City virtually invented "one-stop shopping."

Webb's City sold groceries, clothing, shoes, pharmaceuticals, auto parts (and even automobiles), housewares, furniture, toys, records, carpeting, sporting goods, garden supplies and pretty much anything else you might be looking for (except liquor, which Webb chose to discontinue after the first few years). There were restaurants and there were snack bars, a bakery, a barber shop and a beauty salon.

The eye of the hurricane, James Earl "Doc" Webb, arrived from his native Tennessee with an elementary school education, $5,000 saved up, a satchel full of energy and some very big dreams. It was 1926, just before the Florida land boom went bust. And the wet, black blanket that was the Great Depression.

"He was one of those guys that people told 'It will never work, you can't do this' and that just fueled his fire," observes Rui Farias. "He did it anyway."

Webb, Farias explains, was part smart businessman and part carnival barker. His motto – well, one of his mottos – was "Stack 'em high and sell 'em cheap," and because he bought produce and product in bulk, he was able to do both. Which probably explains how Webb's Cut-Rate Drugs, as it was known until 1946, was able to not only survive but thrive during the Depression.

"He came at a time when the city was exploding with growth," says Farias, "when every schemer in America came to Florida trying to make a buck or two. He didn't just come down here and say 'Let me sell you some swampland.' He used crazy promotional antics, but he was here for the long run. He actually used it to help build the city. He didn't just promote his store; he promoted the city."

Billboards on US 301, US 19 and US 41 advertised "The World's Most Unusual Drug Store," for hundreds of miles in every direction. Webb's advertising included five consecutive full pages in each Sunday's edition of the *St. Petersburg Times*. He brought singers and circus acts in to do shows in the parking lot, and constructed an outdoor amphitheater on the roof. The Arthur Murray Dance Studio rehearsed and performed in the "Roof Garden." Webb himself was known to croon there on occasion.

By promoting Webb's City, Webb was promoting St. Petersburg.

He is credited with the nation's first "express line," for 10 items or less, and with installing the first escalators on Florida's west coast.

It was said – by Webb himself – that Webb's City sold 80,000 pounds of sugar and 22,500 cans of soup in a single day, and 40,000 pounds of fresh meats and 3,600 pounds of cheese in an eight-hour period. Webb claimed to sell an average of 16,000 packs of cigarettes a day.

> *It was said that Webb's City sold 80,000 pounds of sugar and 22,500 cans of soup in a single day.*

Then there were the zany promotions. He sold dollar bills for 95 cents. Breakfast (one egg, two strips of bacon, three slices of toast, grits and ham gravy) cost three cents. Two barely-dressed young ladies lounged in a bathtub full of bubbles, on the sales floor, as Webb shilled for a brand of "sweet-smelling soap." He and his senior staff dressed in hillbil-

Dawn Coffee was Webb's own brand, roasted and ground on the premises. St. Petersburg Museum of History.

ly garb to stage a little skit in which Webb, because of his low, low prices, was sent packing, back to Tennessee. He sold "Florida Sunshine in a Can," and folks bought it. His "Poster Girls," beautiful young women in bathing suits, accompanied him on promotional rounds. That got people's attention.

Fortune Magazine profiled Webb in 1948, under the headline *The $12,000,000 Drug Store!* In addition to buying in bulk directly from manufacturers, Webb's success was attributed to taking advantage of the proffered two percent discount by

Doc Webb and friends, circa 1940s. The parking lot circus was a popular diversion. St. Petersburg Museum of History.

always paying in cash, turning over inventory quickly (thereby avoiding cost markdowns necessitated by an overstuffed warehouse) and keeping the overhead low (Webb himself did not have an office, but stayed on his feet all day, every day).

About 10 years ago, I tried to do it all myself and found it utterly impossible – it nearly killed me. Now, we have managers who are responsible for the operation of the 59 separate stores in Webb's City ... An executive's first function of importance, I feel, is trouble shooting. I expedite. Rather than president, I regard myself as chief executive. I think an executive has to know a little bit of everything in regard to the operation of a store.

In 1926 our store was 15 feet wide and 20 feet long, and the gross sales were $38,000. In 1956, our gross sales were $25 million. Our growth averages 10 to 15 percent a year, far above the national average. Our cash registers ring up 150,000 sales daily.

J.E. "Doc" Webb/St. Petersburg Times, June 16, 1957

In that same issue of the *Times*, Webb's five pages of ads included this (sic):

Being Advertising Director for Webb's City I Probably Deserve More Sympathy Than a Guy With Two Fractured Legs. The Other Day When Things Were Fairly Routine I Had a Warning Call From Mr. Johnson, Our Vice President, Saying Doc Was On the Move Again And Was On His Way To The Advertising Department. Again, I Said. That's a Crock. I've Never In Twenty Two Years Seen That Guy Without That Moving and Remodeling Glare in His Eye. All He's Done Lately Is Tear Down 38 Houses To Make Parking Places For 350 More Cars, Moved the Nursery, Remodeled Plant City, Put in New Bird And Rare Animal Cages, Finished A New Florist Shop, Enlarged And Remodeled The Music Store, Completely Remodeled The Downstairs Cafeteria And Installed New Tile And Rest Washrooms, Remodeled And Expanded The Retail Meat Section Of The Super Market ... Doc Bounded Into The Advertising Department. He Had Passed Up The Elevators He Was In Such A Hurry. "Get Your Pencil And Paper" He Yelped. "I've Got It." I Didn't Know What He Had But I Knew It Wasn't Going to Be Good For Me.

Webb's City was slightly south of downtown proper, in an area of the city with a predominantly Black, and poor, population. Webb had done this intentionally, because the land was cheap, and those 38 houses he bought and razed for his parking lot were "slum shacks with outside toilets," he recalled in the *Evening Independent* in 1972.

Webb had a handshake relationship with St. Petersburg's African American population. Blacks were welcomed in Webb's City – green was the only color he really saw – but as with so many other white-owned businesses of the mid 20th century, there were restrictions on where "they" could shop.

"We were not allowed to eat in

Webb's City was known for its zany promotions, in all departments. St. Petersburg Museum of History.

Webb's City at the counter and restaurant," customer Doreen Baker recalled in the PBS documentary *Remembering Webb's City*. "They had two water fountains, and one was labeled 'colored only,' the other 'whites only.'"

Although nearly 10 percent of Webb's 1,700 employees were Black, in 1960 the NAACP picketed inside the store, insisting that the number was disproportionate to the number of Black customers. A lunch counter sit-in took place on Dec. 2.

I don't understand why this group picks on us. In my opinion we have been among their very best friends in the entire country and I make no apologies for any treatment of the Negro race … I have always appreciated their patronage and have given them the same service I have given to all. We have kept competition keen for them and know that we have saved them many thousands of dollars ... We have thousands of Negro customers and friends throughout the county.

J.E. "Doc" Webb/St. Petersburg Times, Dec. 3, 1960

In 1962, 17 St. Petersburg stores, including Webb's City, lifted all restrictions on lunch counter service. The Civil Rights Act of 1964 made it illegal to discriminate against people because of race, color, religion, sex or national origin.

"It wasn't just a store." When Rui Farias gets talking about Webb's City, he is testifying. "You could go there and spend hours and hours. As a kid, I lived four or five blocks from Webb's City. It was like your playground. I would beg to get my hair cut every week so I could get a free ice cream cone. They had a floor of tourist tchotchkes – shrunken heads and coconuts, and all kinds of weird things made out of shells.

"The fourth floor was the toy department – it was a gigantic toy department, like a kid's dream. You used to be able to test-drive the toys. See what they were and play with them. Then you could buy them and take them home."

The fourth floor was also where the coin-operated "cool" stuff was – the baseball-playing ducks, the kissing rabbits, the duck that banged out "Sweet Georgia Brown" on a toy piano, and the chicken that danced (according to legend, the bird was standing unceremoniously on a hotplate, which switched on when the customer's dime dropped).

And the mermaid cave, with mannequin mermaids (whose apparel, over the years, got scantier, as per Webb's orders). A store employee would innocently ask a visiting child his or her name, and within seconds the "mermaid" was instigating a conversation with the wide-eyed youngster: "Hello, Debbie. How are you today? Have you ever met a mermaid?"

Rui Farias grew up in the late '60s and remembers it all like it was yesterday. Webb's City was already a little long in the tooth – fraying around the edges – but in his mind's eye, it was magical, "like going to an amusement park, without the animals or the rides," he says.

"Two of my cousins and my brother worked at Webb's City growing up. I used to hang out with the mermaid on Saturday mornings, behind the magic glass, while she talked to people.

"I would just pedal on my bike over to Webb's City. My mom would say, just be home for dinner. Nobody even thought twice about that. I don't think we even locked our bikes."

The city's westward expansion, into the suburbs, began to make downtown – and shopping in the old spots – obsolete. By the dawn of the 1970s Eckerd Drugs, J.M. Fields, Zayres and Woolco were seriously eating into Webb's City business. More and more, the aging giant was catering to elderly customers, the faithful holdovers from an earlier time and those living on fixed incomes, and the residents of south St. Pete neighborhoods.

The Department of Health, meanwhile, cited Webb's City for numerous violations.

In 1972 Webb bought and refurbished an enormous building at the intersection of 66th Street and Park Boulevard in Pinellas Park. "Webb's Big Super" performed well at first, but in the end it could not compete with the big-box stores that were cropping up on every other suburban street corner. The location was shuttered after just four years.

Doc Webb had retired by then, stepping down as president and selling his shares in the company he'd built from scratch. Devastated by the death of his beloved wife Aretta, dismayed at the inevitable decline of his empire, and freshly diagnosed with Parkinson's Disease, he gave it all up at the age of 74.

With downtown in an economic tailspin, Webb's City failed under its new management. Times ads blared *Webb's City Needs Cash – Entire Stock ½ Price!*, and the final sale of sales took place on Aug. 18, 1979.

Doc Webb was 85 years old when he died in 1982. The building at 9th Street and 2nd Avenue South, empty and decrepit, was demolished two years later.

Rui Farias teaches Florida History at

> "Hello, Debbie. How are you today? Have you ever met a mermaid?"

Circa 1940s. St. Petersburg Museum of History.

St. Petersburg High School. His students, he says, love to hear him talk about Doc Webb and the "City" that bore his name. They look at him in disbelief and hang on his every word.

"Now, anything's available to them," Farias explains. "You can go to Publix in the middle of winter and get watermelon, from Chile or somewhere.

"I remember when it was a big deal when it was watermelon season, and the trucks would come in and unload thousands of watermelons in the parking lot at Webb's City. And there would be lines of people waiting, because it was the first watermelon of the season. Or when the Georgia peaches came in, by the trainload."

James Earl "Doc" Webb, 1899–1983. St. Petersburg Museum of History.

MARINE ARENA

A photograph in the Oct. 2, 1953 edition of the *St. Petersburg Times* shows five men standing on a dock, a dead bottlenose dolphin stretched out in front of them. They are identified as being from a boat called Dixie Queen, out of Johns Pass:

The porpoise was lassoed but fought so hard he killed himself threshing (sic) against the boat. Other attempts will be made, using new methods planned by the crew.

The fearless fishermen had been in the Gulf that day in response to a bounty placed on "porpoises" by Jack Hurlbut, the proprietor of the Marine Arena, a new Madeira Beach tourist attraction. Two of the animals had recently died in Hurlbut's care, and he was offering $100 apiece for new specimens for his 54 x 24 foot "show" tank.

Until Congress passed the Marine Mammal Protection Act in 1972, it was legal to harass, capture, kill or possess bottlenose dolphins, aka "porpoises."

They're completely different species, of course, but in those days most people didn't know, or care.

Long before Congress acted, marine scientists did know that the animals were hyper-intelligent and sensitive, and thanks to TV's *Flipper*

Jack Hurlbut puts Paddy The Porpoise through his motions for the youngsters. Collection of the author.

and the proliferation of those places where they jumped through hoops and tooted horns for the amusement of tourists, bottlenose dolphins were the subject of fascination.

But they didn't have any rights at all. And back in the '50s, when Jack Hurlbut built the Marine Arena, a porpoise was just another fish to be taken and exploited.

A mechanical engineer with a degree from Duke University, Hurlbut left his native Illinois in 1943 with his new, Florida-born bride. They settled in Madeira Beach, where Hurlbut could indulge his passion for fishing. He bought an old bait shop, right across from the docks, and launched a new career.

"He used to go up on the old Johns Pass Bridge, in the evening when work was over," recalls Hurlbut's son Wayne, now 80 and living in New York. "And he liked to snook fish. And one night he caught 23 snook. I have a hunch that's something close to a world record."

Jack Hurlbut served on the Madeira

1950s: Wilson Hubbard and his captive Sand Key dolphins. Hubbard family photo.

Beach town commission from 1951 to '55.

Jack's Bait Shop, as it was called, came to be known for the unusual local fish Hurlbut kept alive in his baitwells. They were caught from the bridge mostly, or from boats – the waters around Johns Pass were teeming with fish then, and visitors would stop in to gawk at sea robins, flounder, redfish, snook, snapper, rays, sheepshead, small sharks and even the occasional tarpon. His buddies would bring them in alive and drop them at Jack's Bait Shop.

All this attention gave Hurlbut an idea. Alongside the bait shop he constructed, from his own design, a 50,000-gallon concrete aquarium, with 17 small portholes of ¾ inch thick glass, and a viewing area (with bleacher seats) on top. Hurlbut, his wife and their young son lived in the adjacent apartment.

"My bedroom was upstairs, and it was only 15 feet from the tank," recalls Wayne Hurlbut, whose parents called him "Punky" in those days. "Downstairs was the gift shop, where you would buy your ticket. So for a neighbor I had a porpoise, or a dolphin, or whatever you want to call him. Plus a lot of other fish; he had tanks all around the lower level, around the outside of the big tank."

When the Marine Arena opened, on July 4, 1953, there were dozens of fish in that big tank, a 300-pound loggerhead sea turtle Hurlbut dubbed Stinky, a pair of 450-pound Goliath grouper (then known as Jewfish) and a juvenile bottlenose dolphin he named Frankie.

Frankie had been snared in a mullet net on Pass-a-Grille; left by his captors in the sun too long, he was blind in one eye.

Hurlbut's first two sharks beat themselves to death against the sides of the tank. Only the docile nurse sharks, somehow, survived and thrived in the aquarium.

Captive tarpon never ate, and always died.

According to the *Times*, the turtle was sometimes confined to a small steel cage at the side of the tank.

The closed-in roof allowed little sunlight to get in.

Nevertheless, as a curiosity the Marine Arena was an instant success, particularly when Hurlbut began to teach Frankie to do "tricks" for fish.

But there was always drama:

When Johnnie, a larger porpoise brought in to be Frankie's playmate, went berserk and tried to kill Frankie by battering his mid-section with his snout, Hurlbut anxiously paced the rim of the tank until police could be summoned to bring a final halt to the brutal Johnny with several well-placed shots.

St. Petersburg Times/Nov. 17, 1953

Frankie stopped eating and died the next month.

Frankie and Johnnie were replaced in February. Hurlbut had snared one of the new creatures himself, 18 miles offshore, and the other he purchased from the Daytona Beach Sea Zoo, driving it across the state on a salt-water-soaked mattress in the bed of his truck.

What happened next is lost to history, but in December 1954 it was reported that Hurlbut had purchased two more porpoises from local charter boat operator Wilson Hubbard.

One of Hubbard's businesses was an excursion boat to Shell Key, where he and his crew had constructed a pen, from chain link fencing and wood pilings driven into the sand, right there on the remote beach.

Here they kept porpoises they had netted, or snared with a special contraption they'd come up with, to "entertain" guests on their tour boats.

Several times a day, seven days a week, the Shell Island boat would arrive and Hubbard would toss fish to "Mike" and "Patty" (named for his young children) and "Frank" (named for the man who'd helped design the snare).

Hurlbut, meanwhile, went through numerous "porpoises" in 1955, including a pair delivered from Marathon Key by a bounty-hunting married couple. "Johnnie II" was the star of his little show until September, when it was reported that the animal had taken "ill" and had been released back into the Gulf.

When a storm knocked down a section of Wilson Hubbard's Shell Key porpoise pen, "Mike" and "Frank" escaped, leaving "Patty" as the last captive animal. Hubbard, weary of the work and the maintenance, decided to abandon the project. In 1956, he sold Patty to Jack Hurlbut.

Somebody, most likely Hurlbut himself, noticed right away that the newest captive at the Marine Arena was a male. And so Patty became Paddy.

Paddy the performing porpoise spent the next nine years of his life swimming back and forth in that tiny concrete cage, three shows a day, 75 cents for adults and 35 cents for children.

At maturity, the animal measured 7-foot-10 inches from nose to fluke. The homemade tank was 10 feet deep.

Paddy turned out to be easily trainable. Hurlbut, who had no previous experience in such things, worked with the dolphin daily, first on rudimentary "tricks" like leaping on com-

> **Paddy the performing porpoise spent the next nine years of his life swimming back and forth in that tiny concrete cage.**

The Hurlbut family lived in the apartment over the gift shop. Postcard image.

mand, shaking hands or returning a beachball. "He taught that porpoise, or that porpoise taught him, I'm not at all sure how it was," remembers Hurlbut's son. "Dad made this little organ. It had four pedals on it, four different notes. They were different colors. And he actually got that porpoise to play a tune. It took some time ... but I thought it was amazing.

"I went diving in the tank one time. Dad wanted to get the sides scrubbed, so I put an aqualung on and I went in the tank. I was going along scrubbing the walls, and that silly porpoise come up and poked me with his nose. Scared me half to death.

"That's one story that comes to mind. There was a million of them, but I think I've forgotten most of 'em."

Paddy, Jack Hurlbut told the *Times*, was "too smart for words. He actually understands you."

Hurlbut was proud of the clear water at Marine Arena. He'd been fascinated by Marineland, the attraction near St. Augustine, and his original

sketches for the Maderia Beach facility resemble the open-air Marineland in miniature. "That's where Dad picked up some of his information on the filtering systems, and one thing and another," Wayne Hurlbut recalls.

Marineland's filtration secrets were protected by copyright; Hurlbut, his son says, deduced how the system worked and "built it himself" using $20,000 in spare machine parts.

From Florida State University biologist Winthrop N. Kellogg, author of the book *Porpoises and Sonar*, came to the area in 1962 and performed a series of "intelligence tests" on Paddy, and pronounced the aquarium dolphin "the most sophisticated and best-trained porpoise in the world."

(The tests) proved, among other things, that Paddy can outthink and outperform five chimpanzees undergoing duplicate tests – and still do three shows a day in the bargain.

St. Petersburg Times/Sept. 9, 1962

The arrival of the $3.5 million Aquatarium on St. Pete Beach

> **Hurlbut sold Paddy to the Aquatarium in 1966; the dolphin died there the following year.**

spelled the end of the line for Jack Hurlbut's facility, which he had re-christened the Johns Pass Aquarium.

Knowing full well he couldn't compete with the new kid in town and its 1.2 million-gallon, open-air stadium tank, he sold his entire stock – including Paddy, his recently acquired sea lion Sydney, 50 fish and the contents of the gift shop – to the Aquatarium.

Jack Hurlbut continued to operate his bait shop, then went to work as a machine engineer for Brite Industries. He died in 1975, at age 61.

Within a month of his January, 1966 transfer, Paddy was back to three shows a day. Because of his "inability to get along with others" he was kept alone, in a smaller tank away from the attraction's other "performers."

Paddy was found dead in his Aquatarium tank in November of 1967. The newspaper headline read *Paddy Joins His Buddies in Eternally Quiet Sea.*

TIKI GARDENS

On a narrow stretch of sand in the town of Indian Shores, the earth has reclaimed Tiki Gardens. The tidy footpaths that meandered past neatly-manicured palm trees and flowering bushes, grass huts and painted stucco Tiki statues are covered now with greenbrier vines, scrub palmetto and 30 years of the matted, decayed detritus of palm, pine and invasive Brazilian pepper trees.

Once, this was paradise.

The lagoon and canals dredged in the early 1960s are still there, but they're muddy and formless, their limerock borders having caved in long ago. The wooden footbridges are gone. The tide still comes in from Boca Ciega Bay, at the back of the site, but the mangroves and sea grapes, long unchecked, have created a thick and impenetrable wall.

These 12 overgrown acres were home to one of the most popular tourist destinations in Florida. In the pre-Disney era, Tiki Gardens attracted 500,000 visitors annually.

It finally ran out of gas in 1988, and today the property is county-owned, with the paved acreage that fronts Gulf Boulevard serving as a beach access parking lot. Traffic rolls past; families pull in, park and unpack beach chairs and umbrellas, chat-

The enormous "tiki heads" at Tiki Gardens were made of plywood and plaster. Unless indicated, the photos in this chapter are postcard images.

tering happily as they walk across the two-lane road and beeline for the hot white sand of the Gulf.

Behind the chain link fence, however, the only sounds are the rustle of something slithery underfoot, the call of a passing gull and the occasional splash of young fish, spawned in the brackish water between the protective roots of the mangroves.

On so many long-ago nights, the air was filled with the loud bray of peacocks, the whooping of monkeys, and the voice of Frank Byars, the owner and ringmaster of Tiki Gardens, the namesake of Trader Frank's restaurant, on the wind:

Aloha, ladies and gentlemen, we're broadcasting live direct from beautiful, exotic Tiki Gardens, right here from the heart of the gardens. From our broadcast booth, here's Ernie Shreeves on the Wurlitzer, bringing you a beautiful medley of Hawaiian tunes. We're bringing you torch-lighting. We do this each evening at twilight. So we extend to you a most cordial invitation to join with us, just as the sun goes down. Right here at beautiful, exotic Tiki Gardens,

when we bring you the ceremony of the lighting of the torches. Aloha.

(The organist plays "Blue Hawaii," "Aloha O'e," "Beyond the Reef" and "Lovely Hula Hands." Palm trees, presumably, sway. Umbrella drinks are consumed from coconut shell mugs.)

Frank Byars ran away from his South Carolina home at the age of 14, and learned the hard way about the value of a dollar. He was a hard worker. From the day he arrived in the Tampa Bay area in the early 1930s until his death in 1995, at the age of 85, Byars was hustling. "Nothing happens until somebody sells something" was his motto, oft-repeated.

Frank and his bride Jo Miller Byars – they met in Tampa – managed a North Pinellas beach motel and sold her jewelry, crafted from local shells, out of a tiny souvenir shack. In the early '50s, they purchased the property at 19601 Gulf Boulevard, in what was then known as Indian Rocks Beach South Shore.

They called their new souvenir business the Signal House, and in time it became the biggest retail outlet in the area, consisting of several small, themed gift shops selling Oriental clothing, baskets, driftwood and other ephemera ("Truly a phantasmagoria of shoppers' delights!" screamed their bright orange tourist brochure) and a small, florid garden walkway with a South Seas Island theme. Tiki Gardens, as they named it, was just a hook to keep visitors in the shops a little longer.

Frank Byars served on the South Shore Town Council, and as President of the Indian Rocks Beach Chamber of Commerce. He once ran, unsuccessfully, for mayor.

In May 1963, the Signal House was destroyed by fire. Undeterred, the couple made plans to rebuild, enlarging the gardens and making the gift shops part of a central complex that would include a 450-seat restaurant called Trader Frank's.

"We'd always dreamed about the South Seas," Frank Byars told the *St. Petersburg Times* in 1978. "So we researched it to see if there were any other attractions in the state with a Polynesian atmosphere. We found there were none.

"We talked to two or three architects about building it, and none of them wanted to touch it. So we bought some brown wrapping paper, and every morning Jo would draw the pictures on the paper, and the builders would build from that. We built the whole thing that way."

Artist Gordon Keith designed the tiki heads to the Byars' specifications.

Tiki Gardens open March 15, 1964. Admission to walk the scenic "Polynesian Adventure Trail," with its tall, foreboding tikis around every bend, was $1.25 for adults, 50 cents for children.

Admission to the gift shops, of course, was free. It was all part of the Tiki Gardens experience.

We'd like to suggest that someday you take your best girlfriend and your camera and visit our island paradise. Out there you'll find the King's Fish Pond, Fire Mountain – the highest promontory in Pinellas County – thousands of beautiful birds, a monkey village to entertain the kids. We say it's a place to dream a while – beautiful, exotic Tiki Gardens.

America was going through a "tiki" craze in the late 1950s and early '60s, with South Seas imagery and design affecting everything from art and architecture to music and movies. The hospitality industry, naturally, found a way to exploit the exotic escapism presented by the all-consuming fad.

Frank and Jo Byars had never been to Hawaii or the South Seas, but they were swept up in tiki-mania – and Frank, in particular, was quick to realize there was a buck to be made.

They sold a little bit of everything in the gift shops, remembers tiki enthusiast Jon Bortles, who's writing a book about Frank and Jo Byars. "They sold baskets, they sold fine china. Anything Frank thought tourists might want to buy, they sold it. They sold menswear, and not everything had the Hawaiian motif. I have a tie with racehorses on it, and the Tiki Gardens label."

> **America was going through a "tiki" craze in the late 1950s and early '60s, with South Seas imagery and design.**

A native of Clearwater, Bortles remembers visiting Tiki Gardens as a child, with his family. The tiki heads, he recalls, were imposing and scary. It was only after he grew up and started doing research on Polynesian culture that he realized what a strange mash-up Tiki Gardens really was.

"A lot of the decorations were painted and designed by Jo who, bless her heart, probably didn't do a whole lot of research into stuff," he says. "People who are seriously into Polynesian art today look at some of it, and they're scratching their heads."

It was, Bortles says, common practice for movies of the era to blithely blend imagery from different cultures. Tiki Gardens was no exception.

"You've got Polynesian things, but right next to them you've got something from Alaska. Or things from Indonesia. Or African masks. Anything that was considered kind of exotic, nobody really went into the history of it. Hawaii, Tahiti, Fiji, Micronesia, they were all lumped into one group. Frank used to buy masks that were made in South America, and put them up for sale as tiki masks."

A record album, *Exotic Sounds of*

Tiki Gardens: A Fabulous Audio Fantasy, was produced in 1967 and sold exclusively in the gift shop. Prized by tiki collectors today, the limited-edition private pressing is a fascinating time capsule, as Frank (on Side One) and Jo (Side Two) breathlessly describe their "South Seas Island Paradise."

It's part "you are there" audio verité and part P.T. Barnum salesmanship.

Following the horn-blowing, drum-pounding accompaniment to the torch-lighting ceremony, Frank – speaking with a thick Southern drawl – introduces "Direct from the Islands, Princess Carloa," who croons Elvis Presley's "Hawaiian Wedding Song" in a tremulous soprano voice. She is identified in the back-cover credits as Carla Perry.

Thank you Princess, really beautiful. And now, the little wahines are leaving to light the torches in big Tiki Gardens. Here you'll find an island paradise. The lighting effects at night are simply fantastic. You should go out and see 'em. It's one of Florida's major attractions. We call it our Polynesian Fantasy At Night. This con-

cludes our ceremony here in the little garden. We hope you've enjoyed it. It's been our real pleasure to bring you this ceremony. We do this each evening at twilight, in an effort to make your stay in Florida, and your visit to Tiki Gardens, a little bit more pleasant.

And so now, let's get on with the luau! Let's go over to Trader Frank's for one of those delightful teriyaki steak dinners. Let's browse the eight shops, they're all jammed with interesting items from the exotic marketplaces of the world! Let's take a stroll on beautiful Pier Kahiki, or visit the Polynesian Fantasy, beautiful, exotic Tiki Gardens. And as they say in Hawaii, until we meet again, aloha.

Trader Frank's didn't have an elaborate tiki-themed floor show; Ernie Shreeves on the keyboard provided the entertainment at the 450-seat restaurant. He was also a homebuilder and, in the 1970s, a pioneer in the development of solar energy. Shreeves' daughter, Lynn Shreeves Dixon, remembers him as a "jack of all trades."

Dixon was born the year her dad performed on the Byars' souvenir record album. As a child, she had the run of Tiki Gardens. "I thought it was normal, go see Aunt Jo and Uncle Frank," Dixon says. "You had your favorite tikis as you ran along the paths, exploring. Peacocks everywhere. And it was great at night when they had the tiki torches out. It was really magical."

> *"Let's go over to Trader Frank's for one of those delightful teriyaki steak dinners."*

Her parents were friendly with the Byars, who lived just up the road, on the beach side of Gulf Boulevard. "They loved the culture. When we'd stay at their house, they had these little books and I'd read about the gods of Hawaii, and all the different cultures of that area of the world."

Frank and Jo had begun making trips to the island every other year or so. Frank bought up every trinket he could lay his hands on, wholesale, and brought them all back to restock his shelves.

For *Exotic Sounds of Tiki Gardens*, Frank field-recorded "the mating call of the proud peacock" (approximately 50 of the large, loud birds were free to roam the grounds), the wild parakeets in the bell tower, a barking wooly monkey named Chester, the talking mynah birds ("Frank and Jo"), the cooing of doves and the lapping of waves.

On Side 2, Jo took over for more of the same:

On an island, near a windswept beach, lies a little bit of paradise called Tiki Gardens. During the next few moments, we will transport you there by sound, captured on a trip through this land of enchantment. In the background: The theme song of Tiki Gardens, inspired by its romantic beauty. Come with us as we thrill to the exotic sounds of this Polynesian fantasy.

This was Ernie's spotlight, as he played his original composition, "Tiki Gardens Polynesian Fantasy," overdubbing piano on top of his Wurlitzer organ. Strangely, the song is repeated several times, decorated with the same loop of shrieking peacock sounds we heard on Side One, then the monkeys and the doves, and the lapping waves, and seagulls, and what sounds like it's supposed to be an erupting volcano.

The fourth time it comes along, someone has added Hawaiian steel guitar, creating the most islandy-sounding moment on the entire record, classic exotica.

Frank and Jo Byars's only child, daughter Sherry Jo, had died of cancer during the Signal House era, at age 16; they later established a scholarship in her name at Eckerd College. With no family to speak of, they poured everything they had – their time, talents, energy and money – into Tiki Gardens.

"We think of Tiki Gardens as the place to dream awhile," Frank told the *Tampa Tribune* in 1987. "All the other attractions emphasize excitement. Here, people can think about the things that have happened to them, and those that might happen."

Ultimately, like all roadside attraction owners, the Byars were forced to concede that Disney, and the other excitement-generators, were unbeatable. By the 1980s, business at Tiki Gardens was falling off; the tiki craze, of course, had passed into history and was considered little more than kitsch. Hurricane Elena in 1985 left sections of the trail in ruins.

Age was catching up with them, too. It was time to go. Frank and Jo accepted an offer of $2.95 million from a pair of Australian investors in 1988 (including, reportedly, $1 million in rare black opals). They opened a small souvenir shop, Fun & Sun, in Johns Pass Village.

The Australians' attempts at keeping Tiki Gardens operating failed, and in 1990 the property was sold to Pinellas County for $3 million (no opals were exchanged). The tikis, the birds

> **All that remains of Tiki Gardens is a 170-space beach access parking lot.**

In his quest for the tourist dollar, Frank Byars thought of everything. Jon Bortles collection.

and animals, the pontoon boats and the contents of the restaurant and gift shops were sold at auction. The buildings were taken apart and the rest was bulldozed.

Jo Byars passed away in August 1994; Frank followed 14 months later.

At 19601 Gulf Boulevard there's no trace of Tiki Gardens, and the significant role it played in the growth of Pinellas County tourism, except for a small sign at the entrance to the 170-space parking lot that proclaims the area is now known – rather unromantically – as Tiki Gardens Park Beach Access.

Behind the fence, however, there remains a ghostly voice on the twilight breeze. It's Jo Byars.

And now we leave this land of enchantment, intrigue and mystery, hoping someday to return to this paradise, to walk again amongst the giant Tiki gods, who stand majestically guarding the secrets of the past. We say aloha.

LONDON WAX MUSEUM

Jose Gaspar and his pirate pals in a London Wax Museum tableau. Postcard image.

When Rob Stambaugh was a boy, his job was to sweep up the family business every night, once the last customer had departed and the buzzing, backlit sign out front was turned off.

In the early 1960s, Stambaugh's father Ted was the general manager of the London Wax Museum, one of the first tourist attractions on St. Petersburg Beach. So young Rob and his four siblings took turns, driving a pushbroom along the museum's cold terrazzo corridors, and trying not to look at the lifelike figures staring glassy-eyed out at him from their windowbox displays.

"When you're in there, you just don't even want to pay attention to these things," Stambaugh, 70, remembers. "You're just keeping your head down, going back and forth.

"But my dad was a practical joker. He'd sneak into one of the scenes. And he had that ability to know the opportune time to reach out and grab you ... and oh, my God."

A realtor by trade, Ted Stambaugh had been a member of the St. Pete Beach City Commission, and had even served a term as mayor. He was the first president of the St. Pete Beach Chamber of Commerce. He wasn't a native, but had lived in the city since the age of 5, and had seen it grow from a scrappy community of bait shops and seafood shacks along Gulf Boulevard to a home for mom and pop motels, upscale hotels ... and tourists.

The London Wax Museum – "From Josephine TUSSAUD in England"

> *The Chamber of Horrors was Ted Stambaugh's favorite place to play pranks on his children.*

trumpeted the unmissable sign, a replica of London's famous Big Ben - opened at 5500 Gulf Blvd. on the second day of March, 1963. Ted Stambaugh was right there greeting his guests, and he was still there, still playing pranks on his kids and his grandkids, until the museum breathed its last, 25 years later.

Josephine Tussaud's great-grandmother was Marie "Madame" Tussaud, the French artist who established a traveling collection of waxworks in England in the early 19th century. The name Tussaud became synonymous with lifelike wax figures, and Marie's descendants carried the craft into the modern age, expanding as an across-the-pond franchise to Canada and, inevitably, the United States.

Stambaugh the realtor brokered the property deal (approximately one acre between the main drag and Boca Ciega Bay) for Canadian entrepreneur T. Alec Rigby, who owned franchise rights to both the Tussaud museums and Ripley's Believe it Or Not, the nationwide string of "odditoriums" that put the weird and the freakish on display. A veritable 20th century P.T. Barnum, Rigby recognized Stambaugh as an invaluable asset, because of his connections to local politics and community concerns, and a fellow traveler with a similarly innate feel for generating publicity.

Opening day for the 8,000-square-foot attraction was big news. Visitors walked past carefully staged tableaus with waxworks – there were 88 of them at first, at a reported cost of $1,000 each – of historical figures, characters from literature and a dimly-lit "Chamber of Horrors," with gruesome scenes of torture and execution (including an "electric chair" that buzzed, sizzled and lit up blood red when a switch was tripped). The claustrophobic room also included less nightmarish figures of movie creeps like the Wolfman, Jekyll and Hyde and the Boris Karloff version of Frankenstein's Monster.

Predictably, the Chamber of Horrors was Ted Stambaugh's favorite place to play sneak-attack pranks on his children.

John F. Kennedy and his First Lady, Jackie, occupied a prime spot near the entrance, in a White House tableau with another hero of the time, astronaut John Glenn.

There were 88 waxworks on opening day in 1963, at a reported cost of $1,000 each.

The London Wax Museum was located at 5500 Gulf Blvd. in St. Pete Beach. Postcard image.

(At a VIP preview the day before opening, someone observed that Mrs. Kennedy's hair was "all wrong," and in fact resembled that of Albert Einstein. A hairdresser arrived in the evening to re-style Waxy Jackie's 'do into an appropriate bouffant).

After JFK's murder later that year, new president Lyndon Johnson and his wife Lady Bird were added. A Kennedy "memorial" scene was hastily created. And in 1964, the Tussaud Company sent over a "new," particularly bizarre historical tableau – the murder of assassin Lee Harvey Oswald by Jack Ruby, with a horrified policeman watching. This was not Tussaud's finest hour: Oswald, a critic wrote years later, looked as if he were about to break into a song-and-dance routine.

Along with his practical-joker side, Rob Stambaugh recalls, "My dad was kind of a carny guy. He would do all these crazy things to get advertising. When the Beatles were hot, he bought four airline tickets for the wax figures and flew them from New York to Tampa. Then he rented a convertible and drove them around town

Wax likenesses of John F. Kennedy, who was President when the museum opened in 1963, First Lady Jackie Kennedy, and astronaut John Glenn. Postcard image.

– the *St. Pete Times* called him and said 'Ted, are you at it again? Everybody in town is all excited because they think they spotted the Beatles riding around town in a convertible.'"

To stave off the brutal Florida sun, Ted kept the air conditioner at full blast as he drove the faux Fab Four through the St. Pete streets. "He moved fast and said a few prayers," remembers his son.

Visitors ogled W.C. Fields and Jean Harlow, Walt Disney, Shakespeare and Mark Twain, Napoleon, Alexander the Great and Henry VIII, a barroom full of lusty pirates and their wenches, Julius Caesar watching a bare-breasted Cleopatra taking a bubble bath ("We were always hoping the bubbles would recede," Rob laughs), the assembled Allied and Axis leaders from World War II and the somber deathbed of Abraham Lincoln, with the president's chest almost imperceptibly moving up and down as he drew his final breaths.

One of slow-moving St. Petersburg's most popular attractions, "the wax museum made a lot of money in the day," Rob adds. "Especially on rainy days, the hotels would be full and we'd do real well. Maybe 1,000 people a day." At its peak, there were about 125 figures on display.

The exact timing is a little murky, but at some point the St. Petersburg museum – most likely when Rigby assumed full ownership of the Ripley's organization in 1969 – dropped Josephine Tussaud as a namesake, and became, officially, Louis Tussaud's London Wax Museum. Louis, who'd died in 1938, was another great-grandchild who'd trained as a sculptor with the Madame Tussaud organization in Great Britain.

Although he kept the London Wax Museum, Ted Stambaugh became a Ripley's executive, traveling the world to make deals and obtain new exhibits on behalf of thrill-seeking T. Alec Rigby.

Son Rob, meanwhile, earned a degree in hotel and restaurant management from Florida State University. When Walt Disney World opened in October 1971, he was running the Polynesian Resort's food and beverage division.

The arrival of Disney signaled the beginning of the end; how could waxy-faced statues of long-dead historical figures compete with animatronics and thrill rides?

In 1978, Rigby gave Ted Stambaugh, his old friend and valued

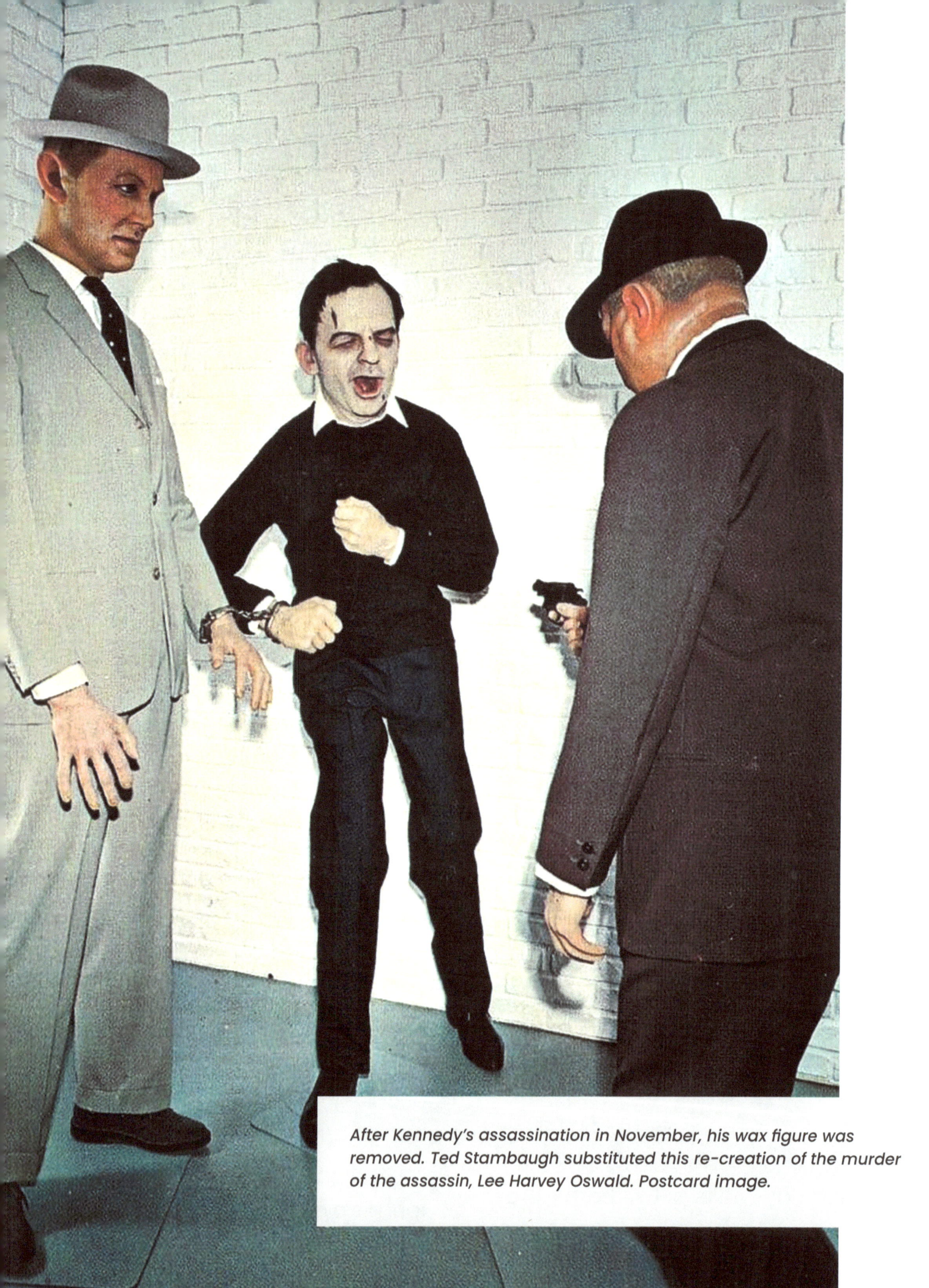

After Kennedy's assassination in November, his wax figure was removed. Ted Stambaugh substituted this re-creation of the murder of the assassin, Lee Harvey Oswald. Postcard image.

associate, a "sweetheart deal" on the Gulf Boulevard acreage. If the writing, however, wasn't yet on the wall – the nearby Aquatarium marine park had recently closed for lack of business – it was becoming clear that tourism was changing at a radical clip. The world was becoming smaller. Rigby was getting out while the getting was good.

Stambaugh, however, was determined to keep his beloved wax museum in operation. He convinced his son to leave Disney and take over management of a derelict restaurant adjacent to the museum. Rob Stambaugh took up the gauntlet and renovated the vacant steakhouse, giving his new place an "Old Florida" theme and naming it after the late Silas Dent, a local legend who'd lived alone on Cabbage Key, near Tierra Verde. Silas Dent, a large man with a long white beard, use to play Santa Claus for the Stambaugh kids, coming in across the bay in a rowboat, at City Hall Christmas parties.

In the 1980s, the three-story Silas Dent's was a massive success. Attendance at the wax museum, meanwhile, was falling perilously low.

"If a person's going to come down to Florida, he's going to go to Mouse Country," Ted Stambaugh groused to the local paper in 1985, further explaining that the London Wax Museum was changing with the times by adding figures of current celebrities like Michael Jackson, Madonna and Rambo, expanding the gift shop and adding a one-hour photo counter.

To make room, some of the less-recognizable wax figures were re-dressed and "repurposed." Lee Harvey Oswald, Jack Ruby and the horrified Texas police officer, for example, would up in three separate Chamber of Horror tableaus.

The end came in 1989. Stambaugh reluctantly closed the wax museum, razed it to the ground, and built a shopping center on the remainder of the property. He died in 1993.

> *Oswald, a critic wrote, looked as if he were about to break into a song-and-dance routine.*

The Caesar and Cleopatra tableau that got Rob Stambaugh so worked up. Postcard image.

"My dad was my best friend," says Rob. 'I wish I had so much of the ability that he had. His vision was just tremendous. He would talk about something, I'd be thinking 'What in the world is he talking about?' and son of a gun if it didn't turn out to be true."

Silas Dent's was gutted by fire in 1996; rather than re-build, Stambaugh sold it and opened a smaller, more compact version at the rear of the property. He sold that place – called Silas' Steakhouse – to Caddy's in 2018.

Today, he and his wife Debbie operate Bayside Banquets, a catering and event company. They lease space on the land that used to belong to the Stambaugh family.

All the wax figures were sold off to

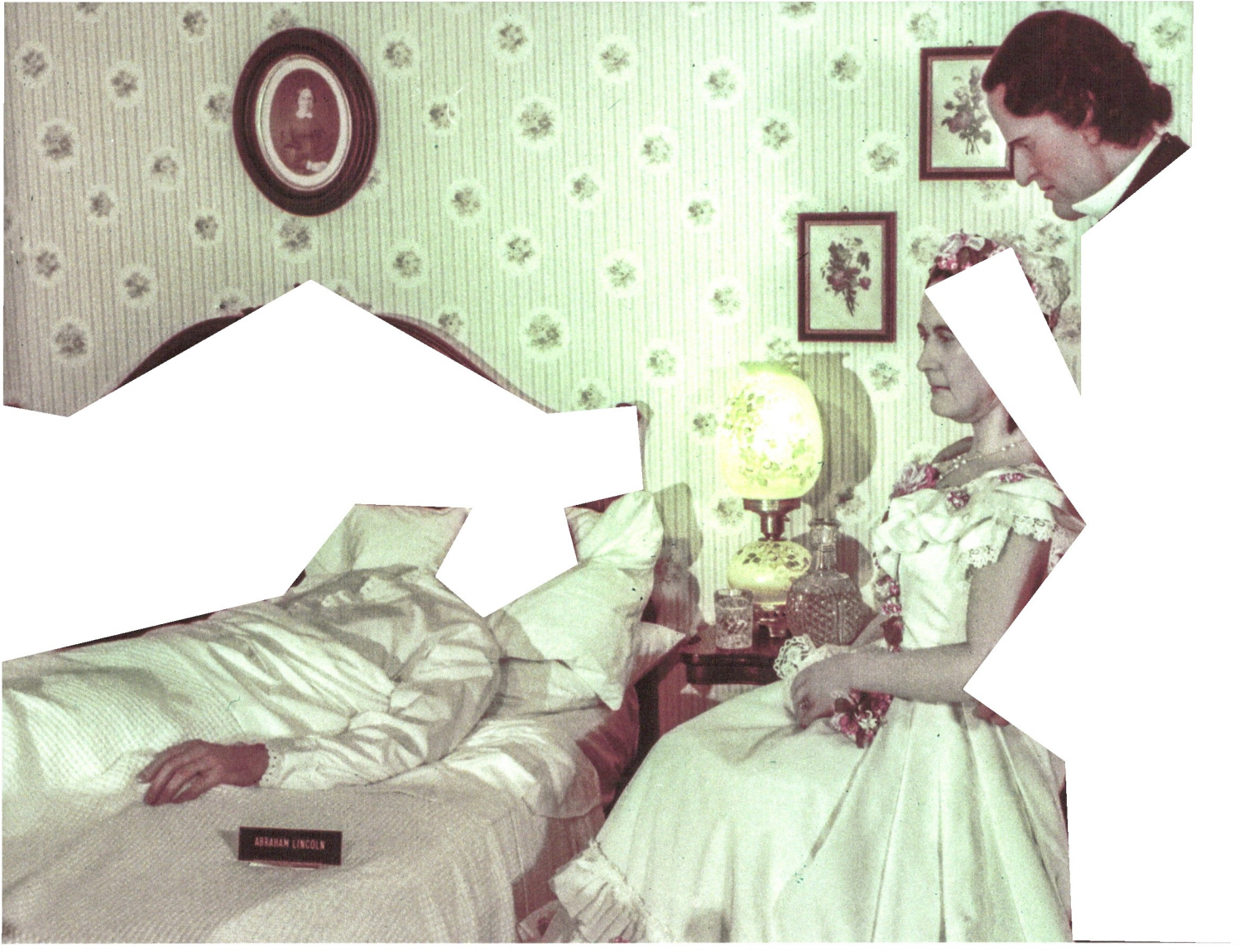

Abraham Lincoln's deathbed scene. The president's chest rose and fell, almost imperceptibly, as he "breathed his last." Postcard image.

other attractions years ago, although Stan Musial's widow bought the wax effigy of the baseball great. Today, the site of the London Wax Museum is an asphalt parking lot next to a T-shirt shop.

But Ron Stambaugh has a thousand priceless memories. Along with boxes of old photos, plastic souvenirs and tourist brochures.

"Some of it, I had put in Silas," he remembers. "It was kind of like a museum with all the stuff I had in there. A slingshot with the wax museum stamp on it!

"I've got a four-car garage that you can't put a car in. Full of stuff. Little by little, I'm re-taking my garage now that I'm semi-retired."

THE AQUATARIUM

Jonah the whale never had a chance.

A 2,000 pound pilot whale, Jonah was the "star attraction" at the Aquatarium, the $3.5 million marine park that opened on St. Petersburg Beach in the summer of 1964. *Flipper,* a series of hit family movies, would soon be all the rage as a Saturday night TV series, and tourists would surely pay good money to see bottlenose dolphins leaping through hoops, tossing beach balls and towing little dogs around on little surfboards. Why not a whale?

Jonah, 16 feet from snout to tail, was netted by a Palos Verdes Marineland crew and sold to the fledgling park across the continent. For two years, the Pacific short-finned pilot whale – a deep-water species not made for swimming in endless circles inside a circular tank 26 feet deep – rocketed out of the water on command, snatching a frozen smelt from the outstretched hand of an employee. That was her "trick," and she did it a dozen times a day.

Animal husbandry, of course, was not exactly fine-tuned in 1964, and in the spring of 1966 Jonah the whale stopped leaping, and stopped eating, and almost exactly two years

The Aquatarium opened on St. Petersburg Beach in the summer of 1964. Postcard image.

after the Aquatarium debuted, she rolled over and died. Jonah was not replaced, and the Aquatarium's dolphins and sea lions continued to captivate record crowds. Her name was not uttered again.

The argument over the captivity of marine mammals, and making them do unnatural things for gawking crowds, has gone on for more than half a century, and will doubtless continue. Pilot whales are no longer kept in tanks for the amusement of tourists; Sea World's treatment of orcas (aka killer whales) has come under intense scrutiny and criticism in the early part of the 21st century.

Political correctness – not to mention moral responsibility – was not on anyone's mind when the Aquatarium opened its doors, on 17 acres right on the beach between 64th and 66th Avenues, on June 27, 1964. The park was developed and bankrolled by South Florida businessman L.G. Ball, owner of the profitable Miami Seaquarium (not uncoincidentally, home of the very animals used for *Flipper*).

Aerial view of the twin tanks. Postcard image.

The doomed pilot whale, Jonah. Postcard image.

A circus atmosphere prevailed, with band music blaring out of the loud speakers, and Aquatarium officials all "spit and polish" in their green uniform coats and gold trousers. There were two shows for customers to see – the feeding of the porpoises and Jonah the whale in the big tank, and performances by the sea lions and porpoises in the smaller tank.

St. Petersburg Times/June 28, 1964

At 1.2 million gallons, the "big tank" was billed as the largest in the world. Over the second, more intimate performance tank, a gold geodesic dome rose 160 feet into the St. Pete Beach skyline, making the Aquatarium one of the area's most instantly-recognizable landmarks, along with the Sunshine Skyway Bridge and the Don CeSar hotel.

Sea water was pumped in from the adjacent Gulf, and filtered before it reached the big tanks.

Scores of local teens and young adults worked at the Aquatarium, from gift shop and maintenance jobs to diving, swimming and feeding the mammals and fish, and crewing the "collection boats" that netted new residents.

Although there were small saltwater aquariums stocked with both indigenous and tropical fish, the emphasis was never on education. Most people just wanted to see the dolphins – over time, and thanks to *Flipper*, the incorrect designation "porpoises" fell out of common usage – leap and play and make those delightful squeaky noises.

After 88 episodes on NBC, *Flipper* was canceled in 1967. The following year, Ball sold the Aquatarium to local hotelier Frank Canova for $2 million.

The bloom, however, was off the rose. "Roadside attractions" that weren't near the Interstate highways – or weren't in Orlando – saw business fall off and eventually collapse altogether.

Canova tried everything. He added a zoological park, with lions and tigers and bears, and in 1975 – in the wake of *Jaws* and the arrival of Sea World in Orlando – changed the name of the park to Shark World.

Nothing worked.

The cast of "performing characters" in the gold tank included California sea lions. Postcard image.

Floppy the dolphin was famous for 25-foot vertical leaps. Postcard image.

Last month, a dispute with the city of St. Petersburg Beach about the construction of a water-slide ride adjacent to Shark World ended with a decision by its owners to close the struggling beachfront tourist attraction.

St Petersburg Times/Aug. 27, 1977

Today, there's no trace of the Aquatarium – or Shark World - on St. Pete Beach. The 17 acres are home to the Silver Sands Beach and Racquet Club.

The Miami Seaquarium bought the dolphins and sea lions, but the sharks, sadly, weren't so lucky. Like Jonah the whale, they were more or less superfluous to human requirements.

"I'm afraid we're going to have to end up destroying them," Shark World trainer Mike Haslett told the *Times* on closing day. "We can't just turn them loose because they're conditioned to eating out of human hands.

"They're not aggressive – they are passive – but we don't want to take the risk of turning them loose and ending up with mass attacks."

MGM'S BOUNTY

hirty-five summers have come and gone since Regan Garnett last stood on the windswept deck of the HMS Bounty, the replica 18th century wooden ship docked for the amusement of tourists at the St. Petersburg Municipal Pier.

Her father was ship's carpenter – he repaired, repainted and replaced every wooden inch of the 180-foot, three-masted sailing vessel, which in those days rarely sailed anywhere more exotic than Tampa, for the Gasparilla Festival "pirate invasion."

Regan Garnett was 12 years old when she and her brother spent that final summer at the Bounty exhibit. "It's funny," she says, "even going into Home Depot now, I smell the Bounty. That wood smell. And it was so hot! They had these big fans in there. All I wanted to do was walk down to the beach and get in the water."

The memories are even more visceral for Tom Boyd, whose own father was captain of the ship and general manager of the exhibit. The Bounty was Tom's second home.

From memory, he can recite the narration that greeted visitors once they'd purchased their tickets, a recording of his dad's voice giving a

June 19, 1965: Accompanied by a flotilla of local watercraft, Bounty makes its grand entrance into Tampa Bay. Postcard image.

simple, easy-to-understand history lesson:

Well, ha-ha, hello there mates. Welcome to the Bounty. Say, have you noticed a special kind of flavor in the air since you came? Why it's oakum, tar, black spruce, oak, pine and manila ... yes, and even old sweat. That's one way of knowin' that you've not come aboard a phony, but a real wind-battlin' timber-shakin' swell-bustin' windjammer. Ah, you could drop a sea-bag in any port in the world, and not see the likes of the ship you're aboard right now. Say, if you've got a minute to spare and are partial to a little yarnin,' I'll tell you why that is. My name's Hugh Boyd, I'm bosun on the Bounty and I've been with this barnacle-bottomed old wind harpy ever since she came down the ways in Lunenberg, Nova Scotia in 1960 and kissed into the Atlantic.

When Tom Boyd was 10, in 1979, his father put him to work. "They had me cleaning the toilets so that nobody thought I was a captain's son," Boyd laughs. "He said 'Well, you can always say you worked your way up from the bottom.'"

In 2012, the ship known as Bounty sank off the Coast of North Carolina during Hurricane Sandy. The then 62-year-old vessel was in the possession of the HMS Bounty Organization LLC, out of Fall River, Massachusetts, which sent her around the world on educational missions, film shoots and promotional tours.

The tragedy, in which Captain Robin Walbridge and crew member Claudene Christian died, marked the final leg of a remarkable journey.

Bounty was conceived in England, midwifed in Hollywood and birthed in Nova Scotia – but the square-rigger's formative years were spent in St. Pete, where up to 250,000 visitors annually took above- and below-decks tours.

Metro-Goldwyn-Mayer commissioned the construction of Bounty in 1960, for use in the filming of *Mutiny on the Bounty*, the second American cinematic treatment of an actual 1789 rebellion aboard a British military vessel in the South Seas.

In MGM's $19 million adventure, Marlon Brando played chief mutineer Fletcher Christian, driven to near-madness by the sadistic captain William Bligh (Trevor Howard).

Never mind that this film adhered to the historical facts even less than the legendary 1938 version, with Clark Gable as Christian, and Charles Laughton as Bligh. Hollywood never let the truth get in the way of a good story.

In 1938, California's Catalina Island stood in for Tahiti and Pitcairn, where the actual events took place. For its Ultra Panavision 70mm Technicolor spectacular, MGM sent actors and crew halfway around the world, to the original locations.

Using the original Bounty plans located in the British Admiralty Archives, a replica – slightly larger, to accommodate cameras, crew and equipment, and with twin diesel en-

> *"You could drop a seabag in any port in the world, and not see the likes of the ship you're aboard right now."*

59

Headed into Tampa for Gasparilla, from left: Jeff Frank Jr., unknown, Tom Boyd, Paul Garnett Jr. and Regan Garnett. Garnett family photo.

gines tucked away – was built in a shipyard in Lunenberg, Nova Scotia at a cost of $1 million. The faux Bounty set sail for the South Seas in August, 1960.

Aboard as an able-bodied seaman was Hugh Boyd, from nearby Dartmouth. Like most of the young crew, he'd signed on because the adventure sounded like heaven: A 'round the world voyage to Tahiti to make a movie with Marlon Brando.

Upon arrival in Tahiti, as a rite of passage Boyd received his first earring. A fellow sailor punched a nail through his earlobe, and sterilized the wound with urine.

As *Mutiny on the Bounty* opened around the country in 1962, MGM sent its million dollar floating baby

The Bounty was moored at the St. Pete Pier for 21 years. Postcard image.

to coastal cities, as promotion. (The film, however, turned out to be a costly flop, and nearly bankrupted the studio).

While Bounty was berthed at the 1964 World's Fair in New York, MGM's marketing chief closed a deal with the St. Petersburg City Council to give the ship a permanent home in the Vinoy Basin, where it would remain tied up near the entrance to the pier as a tourist attraction.

The St. Pete waterfront had a banner '65 - both the Bayfront Center and the Museum of Fine Arts debuted in the spring, and Bounty arrived in June. A "Tahitian village" was created to house the gift shop and administrative offices.

The attraction, officially called MGM's Bounty Exhibit, opened on Friday, July 2. St. Petersburg mayor Herman Goldner gave a speech, and the ribbon was cut by former Miss America Mary Ann Mobley, flown in by the studio for the occasion.

Admission was 90 cents for adults, 50 cents for children.

Hugh Boyd was soon promoted to captain. His assistant exhibit manager, Jeff Frank, had also been on that voyage from New York to Florida, as an engineer.

Frank also managed the all-important gift shop, which turned out to be the real moneymaker. "If we had just depended on the admission alone," he says, "I don't think it would have stayed as long as it did."

Along with representatives from the Aquatarium, Sunken Gardens, the London Wax Museum and Tiki Gardens, Frank created the Pinellas County Attractions Association, so that they could all be marketed under a single banner.

Frank reported 85,000 visitors during Bounty's first six months.

The ante was upped when Walt Disney World opened in 1971. "Disney overall brought people to Florida," Frank believes. "Do they want to spend a whole week's vacation in Orlando, or do they want to come to the Florida beaches? That's something we always struggled with, trying to bring people to the Pinellas County beaches and hence the attractions as well.

"We were never that sophisticated in our marketing to see how Disney drew our customers away from us."

Though she rarely left the dock, Bounty was maintained as a fully operational tall ship. "Gasparilla was a yearly trip, and everybody got so excited because we were actually moving her," Tom Boyd reflects. "We didn't put much sail up in those days, but we had good engines, and Dad was always an expert at picking out good engineers."

> "Hughey knew everything about that ship inside out and backwards and forwards."

Sometimes the crew would get hired out to raise the sails and visit Pensacola, or Fort Lauderdale, as a sort of mobile historical artifact.

Hugh Boyd did a little bit of everything, although he wasn't much for public speaking and conducting tours. He hired more gregarious people to talk to the customers.

"It was a surprising assemblage of skills," his son says. "He's immensely patient, and extraordinarily generous, and really committed to the ship."

"I don't know that he ever realized, but he took his role as steward of this ship in such high regard. And he was always one for restoring it, and bringing it back to its original grandeur."

Recalls carpenter Paul Garnett: "Hughey knew everything about that ship inside out and backwards and forwards. I learned a lot about the way she was constructed in Canada. He was always our link to the past."

Garnett was invited to join the team in 1979, after he'd hand-delivered a stunning 14-foot replica Bounty he'd created in his Boston workshop.

As planking, mast sections or trim cracked or rotted out, Garnett would replace them using – when it was available – the original lumber, and working from the original British blueprints.

Like Hugh Boyd, Jeff Frank, rigger Royd Wheedon and the others constituting the fulltime crew, Garnett took tremendous pride in his ship.

"After she went down in the hurricane," Garnett says, "people were saying 'Oh, well, it wasn't a real ship – it was a movie prop.' I saw red when I heard that. Because she was never, ever intended as a movie prop. The studio had built a ship made to go all the way to Tahiti under her own sail power. And then go around the world on a publicity tour.

"Now, you can't do that on a ship that's just a floating platform. How the hell do you send something like that across an ocean?"

She was, indeed, a real wind-battlin' timber-shakin' swell-bustin' windjammer.

Garnett wasn't able to go on Bounty's biggest adventure, in 1982. Hired out to "play" a pirate vessel in the British/American comedy *Yellowbeard*, the ship motored across the Gulf of Mexico and through the Panama Canal to the shooting locations in Mexico.

His daughter, 9-year-old Regan, had been ill. She wrote him a letter – which he still has – imploring him not to take the trip, and, she admits today, guilt-tripping him.

Tom Boyd went along, however. At 13, he helped out in the kitchen and stood night watch.

Assistant manager Jeff Frank was on the voyage, too, but flew home to St. Petersburg before actual work on the movie began. Although the ship was away, the Tahitian village and the gift shop remained open, and he had to get back to work.

Upon Bounty's return, six months later, things quickly got back to normal.

The Bounty kids resumed their regular weekend routines of hanging around, getting sodas and chips from the vending machines and eating "lunch" with their feet up in the 18-foot longboat display.

An outdoor cage was added to the village, with a quartet of tiny squirrel monkeys inside. "And I had to clean up after the little buggers," Tom Boyd says. "Occasionally, they would get loose – and they were just dying to get over to that ship. They hauled ass and would not be caught."

Regan Garnett: "My dad would be like, 'You guys go sit and do something.' He'd be in the back, carving and painting, and doing other stuff back there. And we'd terrorize the squirrel monkeys. I'd pitch rocks in the longboat. My shoe got stuck in one of the drain holes on the ship and went halfway down."

Garnett later pursued a career in theater, and she is convinced the Bounty was essential training. "I think my being comfortable talking in front of people started in that exhibit," she says. "I had nothing else to do.

"Kids would run around. The parents would try to get the real tour, with Mr. Boyd or whoever was giving the tour, so I'd take the kids and walk around. I'd try to do the same tour. It was like one of my first acting jobs."

In 1985, cable TV magnate Ted Turner purchased MGM, including its legendary film library. He was surprised, the story goes, to find he was also the owner of a fully-operational sailing ship.

The exhibit at the St. Pete Pier was dismantled, and Bounty – still captained by Hugh Boyd – was completely refurbished, including a full set of sails, using Turner money. On Independence Day weekend 1986, it participated in the massive Parade of Tall Ships in New York harbor.

After a trip up and down the Eastern Seaboard, where Turner used the ship to entertain affiliates, he sent it south, where it was moored for three years at a Miami development called Bayside Marketplace.

Hugh Boyd stuck it out for a while, but resigned after the Bayside venture. Frank, Garnett and Wheedon had already bailed.

Turner ultimately donated the vessel to the Fall River Chamber Foundation, which continued to bring Bounty to the Vinoy Basin for the winter months for much of the 1990s. There, without the Tahitian village, the squirrel monkeys or any mention of Marlon Brando, it would be available - a working historical artifact - for visitors to tour.

HMS Bounty Organization LLC bought the ship in 2001, and continued to lease her for film and TV work. Bounty appeared in the second *Pirates of the Caribbean* movie, and in the 2005 big-budget pornographic film *Pirates* (the filmmakers reportedly lied to the ship's owners about the sort of movie they were making).

Then came Oct. 29, 2012. The last photos of Bounty show her foundering and sinking, 90 miles southeast of Hatteras, N.C.

For Paul Garnett, it was like losing a member of the family. "They had done so much to her," he says.

Captain/general manager Hugh Boyd and his son Tom. Boyd family photo.

"To my way of thinking, she wasn't even the Bounty any more. They had changed so much.

"All you have to do is look at pictures or her from the early years, and look at her later – right up to the time they took her out and lost her."

Tom Boyd has a unique way of thinking about Bounty's demise. "One of the more rebellious sailors on the ship decided to paint the bell orange with black polka dots,' he remembers. "And I think about that bell resting on the bottom of the Atlantic Ocean, with a big ol' octopus using it as a carapace.

"That's where I've put her in my mind."

THE PIER

No one in all Florida rejoices more than I in the development of your great city, with its splendid schools and churches … You have added an important milestone in your progress of development, and I have the greatest optimism for St. Petersburg's future, and I predict even greater progress and prosperity.

U.S. Senator Park W. Trammell, former governor of Florida, dedicating St. Petersburg's "Million Dollar Pier," November 25, 1926

There's been one long pier or another on St. Pete's eastern waterfront, extending the local footprint into Tampa Bay, for 131 years. The first one, erected in 1889, was an extension of the Orange Belt Railroad, which was itself something new in the city.

Ships with deep drafts could come into the bay and dock at the 3,000-foot Railroad Pier, as it was known, and its cargo would be unloaded directly into boxcars.

Conversely, St. Petersburg exported three million pounds of fish per year in the 1890s. Processing and ice houses were added to the Railroad Pier, as was a small bath house and toboggan-style slide for recreational use (getting to the Gulf beaches, in those days of palmetto thickets, rattlesnake scrub and crude dirt thoroughfares, was difficult for most if not all of the citizenry).

The so-called "Inverted Pyramid" design, 1973-2015. City of St. Petersburg.

The arrival of another structure, the 1,500-foot Brantley Pier and its roomy bath house, set the stage for a battle between industrial and recreational use. The Brantley Pier was replaced by the Electric Pier, which featured electric lamp lights and ran a visitor trolley along an electrified track. Fishing off the Electric Pier became a popular pastime.

The City purchased several miles of waterfront in 1910, to be used as dedicated park space, effectively ending the battle.

Three years later, the waterfront park system received a new structure, the St. Petersburg Municipal Recreation Pier, strong and sturdy enough to support two-way vehicular traffic. At its zenith was a shaded wooden pavilion, where visitors could sit quietly and watch the birds and the boat traffic on Tampa Bay.

There was an indoor saltwater swimming pool; this structure, a few years later, became the home of the St. Petersburg Museum of History.

The Electric Pier, just 10 feet south of the Municipal, was demolished in 1914. The Railroad Pier would stand,

The Railroad Pier, 1889-1952. St. Petersburg Museum of History.

weak and decaying, until it was taken down in 1952.

The Hurricane of 1921 destroyed the Municipal Pier, and the City set about to design and build a sturdy replacement (also destroyed in the storm was the privately-owned "Fountain of Youth Pier," at 1st Street and 5th Avenue South).

The new city pier had to be something special, too, because tourism – steady, warm weather, beaches and plentiful citrus fruit - was now St. Petersburg's calling card.

It was Lew Brown, the flamboyant editor of the *Evening Independent* newspaper, who began a $1 million fundraising campaign. Brown and his readers raised $300,000 towards the project he called the "Million Dollar Pier," and through a bond issue the City came up with the rest.

And so the "modern era" of city-owned concrete piers began. Extending 1,452 feet into the bay, the new Municipal Pier was formally dedicated on Thanksgiving Day, Nov. 25, 1926, with a crowd of 10,000 in attendance.

It was one of the grandest celebrations in St. Petersburg history as the city's first airfield, named for local

The Electric Pier (night scene), 1905-1914. Postcard image.

developer Walter Fuller, was dedicated on the same day. The 32-acre Fuller Flying Field was located between 22nd Avenue North and Tyrone Boulevard, the site of contemporary Tyrone Square Mall.

The day was filled with parades, band performances, airplane fly-overs and speedboat demonstrations. As it was Thanksgiving, there were public, formal religious services.

The Pier, of course, was the main attraction, as it was something every citizen could enjoy. At the head was a Mediterranean Revival-style casino building, which included a ballroom for concerts, dances and conferences; the office space in the upper level was home to the studios of WSUN, the city's first radio station (WSUN-TV, the first TV station, broadcast from the pier between 1952 and 1970).

Spa Beach was dredged from the bay bottom, created as the downtown alternative to the far-away Gulf shore.

Both beach and pier were fully segregated at the time (as had been the "spa" saltwater swimming pool); in fact, it would be 1959 before Blacks were allowed to partake of either.

The Municipal Pier (aka the Million Dollar Pier), 1926-67. City of St. Petersburg.

In 1930 a roofless solarium, for discreet, gender-separated nude sunbathing, was constructed adjacent to the pier.

The stone, roofless building resembled an Egyptian temple and bore a likeness of the sun god, Ra. Images of snakes and birds decorated the edifice, known as the Temple of the Sun. Admission, locker, soap, a towel and shower cost 35 cents. Once inside, guests discovered numerous chairs and benches amid pure white sand. Capacity was 500 people, and the Solarium averaged 400-600 guests daily in season.

St. Petersburg: An Oral History, Scott Taylor Hartzell

In 1961, despite the addition of modern amenities, including private showers and massage rooms, public disinterest forced the Solarium to close. It was right around this time, too, that civic and community voices began to call for replacement of the outdated, dirty "Million Dollar Pier."

The wrecking ball came for the casino structure in January, 1967.

St. Petersburg was struggling with a serious image problem in the late 1960s; the perception that it was "God's Waiting Room," a dull, sleepy hamlet where old folks lived in trailer parks, napped in the palm tree shade and played 24/7 shuffleboard, had permeated the national consciousness. There was, to be precise, absolutely nothing cool or exciting about St. Petersburg.

In short order, city officials order the removal of the trademark green benches that dotted downtown (not a moment too soon for Black residents, who considered the once off-limits benches unpleasant symbols of the city's segregated past).

Money was secured for a newer, more contemporary pierhead design.

Architect William Harvard got the contract for his "Inverted Pyramid," which was wide on top and narrow at the bottom. The idea, he explained, was to give those at ground level a better and less-obstructed view of Tampa Bay.

Plans called for the five-level, $4 million project to debut during the 1970-71 winter season; delays and cost overruns pushed it back to 1973.

The ribbon was cut on The Pier, as it was called, on a chilly Saturday afternoon, Jan. 13. After a short opening-day parade down Central Avenue from 7th Street, a crowd of "several hundred" (according to the ever-pithy *Times* columnist Dick Bothwell) watched the dedication ceremonies from the sunny side of the street:

Emcee Marshall Cleaver introduced the Stockdales – Adele and Julian – who will provide entertainment in The Pier's Brassaloon starting today. Real troupers, the daughter and father, on organ and guitar respectively, led the crowd in "When the Saints Go Marching In," with enthusiastic hand-clapping to warm numb fingers. One thought of USO shows in Alaska.

The public was allowed in starting Monday, Jan. 15. The Pier included four restaurants, a cocktail lounge and an ice cream bar, all managed by the Marriott Corporation, plus

The "new" St. Pete Pier, dedicated in 2020. Julie Palermo/Aerial Innovations.

shops, meeting rooms and the requisite baithouse for anglers.

A tram called the Pier Tug made the rounds from the waterfront to the pier head for those who did not care to drive, or walk.

Bayfront Center manager Al Leggat, whose nearby facility was also city-owned, gave Bothwell some good news in June. "Here at the Bayfront, we had 883,000 patrons in a year – October 1971 to October 1972. In half that time, The Pier drew almost as many. You know, for the first time in history the city's making quite a bit of money from the pier."

By 1978, however, The Pier's fortunes were already fading. Repairs to the eroding understructure, from exposure to salt water, came to $500,000. Marriott was replaced by the Hardwicke Corporation, which turned one of the restaurants into a disco.

The *Times* reported that year that the City of St. Petersburg would have to subsidize the operation with $177,000 to keep it solvent.

Under consideration was a proposal by an Orlando consulting firm to modify the waterfront area into "Pier Park," with a country fair-type atmosphere including a floating restaurant, rides and games, a botanical garden and more.

"The trouble with downtown is that it isn't thought of as a place to go," said city community development director Bruce Hahl.

"I don't want to give another penny to outside firms when we could do the work ourselves," councilman Dick Martin said.

Mayor Corrine Freeman was in favor of the overhaul. "The only way the pier is going to be successful is people using it," she explained. "Tearing it down is not the answer. With the expertise of these consultants, we should be able to have something creative and attractive."

Meanwhile, the St. Petersburg Police Department assigned extra foot patrol officers to the pier, "to ward off drunks and other undesirables hanging around," according to the *Times*.

Despite numerous overhauls, some of them expensive and many more of the simple, Band-Aid variety, The Pier, with its long-outdated Brady Bunch look, stood sentinel over Bayshore Drive and the bay until 2013, when the city finally shuttered it; it was taken down two years later, at a cost of $15 million.

The Columbia Restaurant, Cha Cha Coconuts and Johnny Reno's Waterfront Restaurant & Watering Hole were no more, and the smattering of shops that remained, four decades after the Pier's debut, faded into nostalgia.

The next step in this long civic adventure began July 6, 2020, when the new $92 million pier opened, during the Covid-19 pandemic. With four restaurants, several recreation areas and more greenspace than many city-owned parks covering 26 acres, it is now referred to as the Pier District.

The Pier represents something special to the people of the Sunshine City. It's an integral part of our skyline. It's long been a fundamental St. Petersburg icon. So I understand the importance of the Pier to the people of this city.

St. Petersburg mayor Rick Kriseman, May 14, 2014

CAPONE, THE BABE AND THE GANGPLANK

The Gangplank and Jungle Prado, circa 1939. State Archives of Florida.

"When the legend becomes fact, print the legend."

So declared a savvy newspaperman in the film *The Man Who Shot Liberty Valance*, explaining that once a tale has been repeated over the years it tends to get larger, taking on mythic proportions, until it grows far more interesting than the original truth.

Stories have circulated for a century about Al Capone and Babe Ruth, two famous figures in American history, and their ties to the area of western St. Petersburg known, in different eras, as The Jungle, Jungle Prada and Jungle Terrace.

Capone, the notorious Chicago gangster, and Ruth, perhaps the greatest baseball player of all time, both certainly visited St. Pete in the early 20th century. As a member of the New York Yankees, Ruth was here every spring training season between 1925 and 1934. His exploits in the city – as a beloved and approachable celebrity, a humanitarian and a prodigious consumer of food and liquor – are well documented.

Capone invested in St. Petersburg real estate, and his bootleg alcohol certainly made its way here during Prohibition, but over time the facts of his local connections have been distorted – if not into the stuff of legend, then into some pretty snappy conversation starters.

The Capone and Ruth stories merge at 1700 Elbow Lane North, three narrow and nondescript acres of scrubland between Park Street and Boca Ciega Bay. What is now known as the Jungle Prada Tavern began life in 1925 as a nightspot (and speakeasy) called the Gangplank. It was the first nightclub in St. Petersburg.

> *Did Capone have a financial stake in the Gangplank? Probably not.*

"People who come in know there's a lot of history of the place," says lead bartender and inventory manager Schawn Williams. "Everybody's like 'I heard Al Capone owned this place,' and a few people bring up what's supposed to be a mysterious safe."

The fact is that the Gangplank was built in 1924, during the Florida land boom, by landowner and developer Walter Fuller. It sat at the Park Street end of a small shopping complex and motel he called Jungle Prado, designed in the Spanish Mediterranean style with high arches, minarets and colorful tile inlays. It was named after Havana's Paseo del Prado promenade.

> **The Bambino certainly frequented the Jungle Hotel and its adjacent golf course.**

At the same time, Capone's "business partner," Johnny Torrio, wintered in St. Petersburg – his wife's family lived here - and engaged in land speculation. He and Capone were shareholders in the Manro Corporation, which bought up approximately 50 acres all over the city, including a large parcel of northern Pass-a-Grille.

According to an *Evening Independent* story from 1965, Capone spent exactly two days in the city in 1926. Other sources say it was 1927 or '28. It's not known where he stayed, although it might well have been Fuller's Jungle Country Club Hotel and golf course, just up Park Street from Jungle Prado and the Gangplank. Torrio was an associate of Fuller's, and he frequented both the hotel and the nightclub.

Fuller operated a dirt airstrip to the east, at the current site of Tyrone Square Mall. Presumably, this is where the vacationing northern swells - and shady underworld figures - would land before proceeding to his hotel, country club and gin joint.

Writing in the *Northeast Journal*, historian Will Michaels speculated that Capone might have been in the city again in 1931, before making his way to the sponge docks in Tarpon Springs. The latter visit was documented in the local papers, while there's only a small, vague mention of the former. "Surely Capone's arrival would have been a newsworthy event," Michaels wrote. "With his extensive facial scars he would have been hard not to notice."

Al 'Scarface' Capone, reputed king

Al Capone, left, and Babe Ruth. State Archives of Florida.

of Chicago's gangland, paid a visit to Pinellas County Monday, spending a few hours in St. Petersburg and later motoring to Tarpon Springs, where he spent considerable time looking over the sponge industry. Capone, with a party of five, including one woman, was seen here by several persons. Later in the afternoon, a large crowd gathered at the Sponge Exchange in Tarpon Springs to see the famous baronial head of the beer racket. Capone's business on Florida's west coast could not be ascertained, but there was plenty of speculation.

St. Petersburg Times/Feb. 10, 1931

Did Capone have a financial stake in the Gangplank? Probably not. In fact, he likely never set foot in the place. The legend, however, is bolstered by stories of a mysterious underground tunnel leading from the property's dock, under the fireplace and into the Gangplank bar.

The bay was wild then, and under-patrolled. It would have been a cinch for Capone and Torrio operatives to offload illicit hooch and run it directly into the nightclub, which at its wintertime peak was the center of action for St. Pete's wealthy visitors. It's said that both Count Basie and Duke Ellington played the club during its heyday. A trolley ran between the club and Fuller's three-story Mediterranean Revival style hotel at the corner of 9th Avenue.

Prohibition was a fact - and the tunnel stories have been passed down from one lessor to the next (a procession of restaurants have called the location home over the decades). Williams swears he can hear a hollow sound when he stomps on a certain section of the entryway floor, which has a small, odd slope – and that the restaurant's current owners were told the city filled them in long ago. He's never seen an actual tunnel. There is no "hidden entry" beneath the fireplace, as legend has often claimed. At least, not one that Williams can find.

"And I've been out there by the bay, looking around for where the entrance might have been," he explains. He hasn't been able to locate that, either.

Fuller's Jungle Country Club Hotel was sold to Admiral Farragut Academy in 1945. The military school sold off the golf course and smaller buildings.

It's likely, too, that there was another bootlegging tunnel, or tunnels,

Jungle Prada as it looks today. St. Pete Catalyst.

> **Jungle Prada's "Capone safe" was opened on TV in 2012. It was empty.**

running under Park Street from the bay to the Jungle Hotel.

In 1970, Fuller confessed – sort of. "I, a nondrinker at the advent of Prohibition became a lawbreaker, a habitual evader of authority, and a steady customer of alcoholic beverages," he said, according to Michaels. "The first bootlegger I ever saw was me. In such an atmosphere, even the most righteous lacked the courage to speak out, and law enforcers became a lonely and ostracized group."

As for the "safe," Williams swears he was told it actually dated from the 1970s, not the Capone/Torrio era, but it disappeared a few years ago – when Jungle Prada Tavern was known as Max and Sam's ... or was it the Saffron's era?

In 2012, the safe was opened on a nail-biting episode of the Discovery Channel series *American Treasures*. Much like "Al Capone's vault" when Geraldo Rivera cracked the door on prime-time TV back in the '80s, the safe was empty.

As for Babe Ruth, the Bambino certainly frequented the Jungle Hotel and its adjacent golf course, and he was known to enjoy certain delicacies at the Gangplank.

Legend: "Babe Ruth got married at the Gangplank!"

Fact: On April 17, 1929, Ruth married Claire Hodgson, his second wife, in New York City. Upon the happy couple's return to St. Petersburg, so the Babe could report back to spring training, they threw a lavish wedding reception at the club.

Ironically, just across the Jungle Prada Tavern parking lot, there is real, verifiable history. Near the site of the remains of a Tocabago Indian village, Spanish explorer Panfilo de Narvaez and his crew of 300 landed in 1528, and from the spot began Europeans' first inland exploration of North America.

The Jungle Prada site - encompassing the Narvaez landing site and the adjacent Tocabago mounds - was added to the National Register of Historic Places in 2003.

Self-portrait in wood by Earl Gresh, date unknown. St. Petersburg Museum of History.

THE EARL GRESH WOOD PARADE

Visit the world's most unique museum ... Thrill to amazing artistry and craftsmanship in rare woods – magnificent murals, furniture, clever and unusual gifts. Pay a visit to pleasure you'll profit by ...

Florida Speaks magazine ad, 1951

The announcement in 2020 that St. Petersburg's Melting Pot fondue restaurant had closed for good led, perhaps inevitably, to a closer examination of the quaint, English cottage-style building that housed the place for 32 years, and its place in St. Pete history.

Before the Melting Pot moved into 2221 4th Street North in 1988, it was the home – for about 11 months – to a restaurant called Iggy's Place. Prior to that, it was briefly called the Stateside Restaurant.

Many will remember it as Rollande et Pierre, the fancy French eatery owned and operated by Rollande Lohrer and her husband Peter, aka. Pierre. Rollande et Pierre was at that 4th Street address between 1959 and

1985.

Although it's been renovated, restored and re-fitted numerous times, the unusual three-building compound was built from scratch in the 1930s by Earl Gresh, a colorful St. Petersburg figure who first achieved fame as an orchestra leader, then as a racing boat champion, a trophy-winning fisherman and - in those bully years between the world wars - a renowned woodcarver and craftsman.

Earl Gresh's Wood Parade – a combination museum, workshop and gift shop – was a top St. Petersburg attraction for 20 years. It was featured in national magazines, on radio and on TV, and in promotional material aimed at attracting tourists to the area, alongside sparkling sunny beaches, juicy oranges - and Sunken Gardens, which was just a few blocks away. There were postcards, too.

The Wood Parade museum opened on Jan. 13, 1940. Admission was 25 cents. "Contains the most varied and complete collection of woods ever assembled," proclaimed the advertisement in that morning's *St. Petersburg Times*. "There are panels of representative woods from almost every part of the world – from Asia, Africa, Europe, Australia and the Americas."

From the handout brochure:

The architecture of Kent, England was chosen for the main building because it offers the best opportunity for displaying the work of wood crafttsman (sic). The building with its mullioned windows is fashioned of longleaf pine timbers with flitch tide-red cypress siding. The riveted shingles of heart cypress are similar to those originally used on George Washington's home, Mount Vernon. Bricks from historic Fort Dade at the mouth of Tampa Bay were used for the garden wall and the immense chimney. The art of the handcraftsman is manifest in every detail of the exterior and interior of the building.

The centerpiece of the museum was a cross-section of an ancient cypress tree; weighing three tons, and measuring 11 feet across at the base, Gresh claimed the wood was 3,000 years old. The tree had been cut down in 1904 near Shamrock, in Dixie County.

He had carved small people, historical figures from across the centuries, and inserted them into the tree-ring timeline.

Yet the real attraction was Gresh himself. He had already made his name as a woodcarver, creating buttons, bracelets, belt buckles, tackle boxes and fishing lures out of his cramped homemade workshop on the 4th Street property. He began to craft ladies' handbags out of soft woods (using cloth interior), and the Earl Gresh Original Wood Purse – patented in 1943 – caught on, selling thousands via mail order.

Visitors came from all corners to view Gresh's hand-carved "paintings in wood" depicting, in more than a dozen separate scenes, the Life of Christ. Using the inlay technique known as marquetry, Gresh created the complex 5x5 foot murals, utilizing 62 different woods, over a span of 17 years.

Earl Parker Gresh had become fascinated with carving soft woods while working at his father's cigar factory in Bordentown, N.J.; he was hypnotized, he always said, by the aromatic smell of the cedar used for cigar boxes. Earl was an ambitious kid - at his military prep academy, he mastered the violin and led the school dance band.

In 1911, when he was 15, he moved with his widowed mother to St. Pe-

tersburg.

After a stint in the Navy during World War I, he returned to St. Pete ... and fate intervened.

"One night by the old wooden pier, I ran into these six boys from Kentucky State College who had an orchestra," he recalled to *Times* columnist Dick Bothwell years later. "I told them I played the fiddle ..."

Soon, the smooth-talking violinist was the Kentucky Kernels' bandleader. A regular booking at the Park Street speakeasy the Gangplank gave the group its new name: Earl Gresh and the Gangplank Orchestra. St. Petersburg's first radio station, WJBB (later WSUN), broadcast several hours every week from the Gangplank, and from the neighboring Jungle Hotel. Gresh, through this association, became the station's first announcer.

The group was also the favored dance band at the Gold Dragon nightclub, high above Rutland's Department Store at 5th and Central.

Between 1924 and 1927, Earl Gresh and His Gangplank Orchestra cut more than a dozen 78s for Columbia Records; this allowed them to tour the country, which they did, until Gresh's wife – home in St. Pete raising their two young sons – insisted he put a stop to it.

He put a stop to it.

Restless at home, Gresh turned to boat motor repair, and then to boat racing. He carved and cured wood to create sleek hulls, which, when motorized, sliced through the waters of Tampa Bay at lightning speeds. A *Times* article dated Jan. 3, 1931 describes him as a "daredevil," entertaining visitors to the downtown pier in his speedboat Hurricane.

Gresh became a national champion speedboat racer after winning 42 consecutive races in the 1929-30 season.

This, unfortunately, dovetailed with the Great Depression, and the boatbuilding and racing businesses stopped paying. So he began to fine-tune his woodworking skills. "Great-grandfather was a wonderful woodworker," Gresh would tell Bothwell. "Grandfather built his home and all of his furniture in Hutchinson, Kansas."

Fishing was Gresh's true love (second only to Marian, his devoted wife). He made and sold custom lures and carved compartmentalized tackle boxes by hand. He fished every river, lake, trout stream, bay, gulf and

Gresh working on his "Life of Christ" murals. State Archives of Florida.

Gresh trademarked his famous line of wooden handbags in the 1940s. St. Petersburg Museum of History.

estuary in the United States. He ran into President Herbert Hoover at Yellowstone National Park – both were there in search of trout in the Madison River.

Gresh taught the president how to tie his own flies, and continued to send him Gresh-made lures for years afterwards. He even made a special tackle box for Hoover. He did the same for Dwight D. Eisenhower, after First Lady Mamie wrote him a personal letter requesting one for her husband.

He founded the local Rod and Gun Club, and was the president of the Propeller Club, and was one of the driving forces behind the Suncoast Tarpon Roundup – the now 85-year-old organization still hands out the Earl Gresh Sportsmanship Award.

The ribbon was cut July 19, 1955 on the last Pinellas County stretch of U.S. 19, connecting south and north. This was the death knell for most tourist-dependent businesses on 4th Street, as the traffic coming in over Gandy Bridge – or the newly-erected

Sunshine Skyway Bridge - was now diverted to the highway.

The Earl Gresh Wood Parade was a casualty of progress.

"This is the end of an era," Gresh said in a newspaper interview. "People don't come in ... it's my hope that some group of businessmen will take over the Wood Parade for exhibit on U.S. 19."

He was asked what he was planning for his "retirement" phase. "I'm interested in testing and evaluating fishing tackle, boats and outboard motors," Gresh replied. "I'm fishing twice a week – wonderful medicine. And I'm designing a set of top water bass bugs for a national manufacturer."

On May 4, 1958, the contents of the Earl Gresh Wood Parade were sold at auction. Gresh donated the "Life of Christ" murals to Memorial Park, the cemetery and mausoleum on 49th Street North, where they are still on display today, inside the Christ Chapel.

Rollande et Pierre moved into the 4th Street property in early 1959.

Marian, Gresh's wife of 55 years, died in 1969. That same year, two of their three sons suffered fatal heart attacks.

> *"I'm fishing twice a week – wonderful medicine," Gresh said when he closed up shop in 1958.*

"I was lost, but I didn't let it get me down," he said. "I believe every day is a new venture, something to look forward to. I'm privileged to be on this earth."

Earl Gresh died June 30, 1977. He was 81.

Writer Jeff Klinkenberg, just a few months into what would become a nearly 40-year career at the *Times*, conducted the last interview with the legendary jack-of-all-trades.

Gresh made it clear what activity had clearly meant the most to him, from his long life and multiple careers.

"Don't write a history of Earl Gresh," the old man, suffering from severe arthritis, said to the young reporter. "Don't. But say this ... here's how to begin the article. 'With Earl Gresh, fishing was a way of life.'

"It really was, you know."

FORT DE SOTO AND FORT DADE

Actor Henry Fonda, lured to the area with the promise of a day's tarpon fishing, gave a short speech at the Fort De Soto Park dedication ceremony on May 11, 1963. Guy Lombardo and His Royal Canadians performed, and 13 local girls competed for the title of Miss Fort De Soto, afterwards posing for photos with an uncomfortable-looking Fonda. There was a waterski show, direct from Cypress Gardens, to hold the interest of the estimated 15,000 locals gathered on yet another miserably hot Saturday afternoon.

Fonda, for reasons lost to memory, arrived with a handful of dirt from Wyoming, site of his most recent film, *Spencer's Mountain*. While news cameras clicked, he poured the soil into a silver chalice, where it was ceremoniously mixed with beach sand, along with what was described as "sand from Spain" by a re-enactor dressed as 16th century Spanish explorer Hernando de Soto, namesake of the park.

Fort De Soto, in reality, had about as much to do with the Spanish, and de Soto himself, as it did with Henry Fonda and his latest box office hit.

Twelve-inch mortars from the Spanish-American War remain at Battery Laidley, the centerpiece of Fort De Soto Park. St. Pete Catalyst.

Every St. Petersburg kid since 1962 (when the first toll road opened) has fond memories of Fort De Soto, a 1,000-acre water-and-woodland park on Mullet Key, the southernmost barrier island off the Pinellas coast. The county acquired the property in 1948 from the U.S. Army Air Corps, which had been using it as a test-bombing range during World War II.

It remains the wildest place in Pinellas, with none of the skyscraping condominiums or other signs of human expansion that spread like fungus over nearby Tierra Verde. It is the domain of raccoons, wading birds, seagulls and sunburned tourists. The kiddie train rides, the beauty pageants, the pomp and the circumstance are long gone; otherwise Mullet Key, and Fort De Soto, look almost exactly as they did the day the park first opened. In Florida, that's saying a

This gasoline-powered "steam engine" train was designed as a miniature replica of the working train that ferried supplies and equipment between the Fort De Soto shipping dock and the military outpost itself. Postcard image.

lot.

The public beach at Fort De Soto is considered one of the best in the state, if not the entire country. In 2009, Trip Advisor named it America's Top Beach.

The beach was always the draw, of course, but in earlier times it had been accessible only by boat. With the coming of the bridge and the public park and Henry Fonda and Guy Lombardo, the expansion of the campgrounds and the construction of a snack bar and a gift shop, Fort DeSoto became part of the "Holiday Isles," Pinellas County's beach-vending marketing blitzkrieg. The door was opening wide for tourists.

At the heart of the park stand the decaying remains of Fort De Soto itself, constructed by the Army between 1898 and 1900. In truth, what every visitor sees – and every easily-impressed local kid vividly remembers – is what's left of Battery Laidley, which housed eight 12-inch mortars, guns that could fire shells up to seven miles. Four of these massive weapons, long since deactivated, are still there.

A series of roughshod artillery and storage rooms constructed from a mixture of seashells, sand and concrete – the walls were between eight and 20 feet thick – Battery Laidley was camouflaged behind a mountain of carefully-laid sand and vegetation, so that enemy ships attempting to enter Tampa Bay, and surprise the all-important Port of Tampa, would not know the Fort, and its guns, were waiting for them.

The Spanish-American War was over in less than a year, and although the resident soldiers conducted numerous drills, lobbing shells at a target towed behind one of their own ships, the fort's guns were never fired at an enemy.

There were, to be sure, enemies everywhere:

The suffering of the men daily at work or drill has been greater than can be imagined by any who have not actually experienced it. There have been nights that the men have had no sleep due to mosquitoes in quarters, even though mosquito bam (nets) are used. At present, life for the men is a torture both night and day, and the mosquitoes have to be fought with a bush continuously whether at work or resting.

Post quartermaster's report, 1908

A second, smaller battery was installed closer to the beach, which allowed a tighter mortar trajectory into bay waters. Erosion has taken a toll on Battery Bigelow, however, and only a few crumbling concrete footers and chunks of wall remain.

Indeed, there's virtually nothing left of the actual Fort De Soto military post, which featured 29 wooden buildings including barracks for the 125 troops, offices, stables, a kitchen and mess hall, a bake house and nice homey quarters for officers and their families.

> *There's virtually nothing left of the actual Fort De Soto military post.*

It's less commonly known that Fort De Soto had a twin, approximately two miles southwest as the

In the early 1960s, there was another train at Fort De Soto. This one zipped through the scrub palmetto and mangroves. The "wild" areas across the main road from the fort. Postcard image.

pelican flies, on Egmont Key. Fort Dade (named for Major Francis L. Dade, killed in the Second Seminole War) actually housed more soldiers (about 250) and included a tennis court, baseball, bowling, a gymnasium and a movie theater.

Because it's never been accessible by car, Egmont Key has remained off the beaten tourist track. The 328 acres of sand and scrub is overseen by the Florida Park Service, and because of its importance as a seabird nesting site, it's also a National Wildlife Refuge. A good part of the island is off-limits to visitors.

Its location at the mouth of Tampa Bay made Egmont a strategic navigational hub for centuries (the first lighthouse was erected in 1848). During the Civil War, it was home base for Union soldiers fearing Confederate blockade runners. It also has historical significance as the site

Ruins of Fort Dade, Fort De Soto's twin, on Egmont Key. Florida State Parks.

of an internment camp for Seminole Indians. The Tampa Bay Pilots Association, which discharges local pilots to navigate incoming cargo ships safely through Tampa Bay, runs a way station on the island.

What's key about Egmont Key is that it was, and is, adjacent to the historical shipping channel, the only way for larger vessels to enter the bay, and reach the port. Any enemy ship – Confederate, Spanish or otherwise – had to pass directly between Egmont and Mullet Keys to get to the centers of commerce and population.

With Fort De Soto on the north side of the channel, and Fort Dade on the south, the bay, the port, the cities and the citizens would be protected.

Of course, protection was never necessary, and both Fort De Soto and Fort Dade were decommissioned; both were completely abandoned by

Two of Fort Dade's rusting 17-ton mortars were "rescued" in 1980, cleaned up and put on display at the Fort De Soto site. St. Pete Catalyst.

the military in the early 1920s.

Although Fort De Soto came back to life as a recreational area, before and after its rekindled military use in the '40s, the more remote Fort Dade was allowed to fall into disrepair; indeed, as Egmont's western coast has eroded, many of the battery buildings have crumbled and/or disappeared beneath the green Gulf waters.

Battery Laidley was listed in the National Register of Historic Places in 1977. Two of Fort Dade's rusting 17-ton mortars were "rescued" in 1980, cleaned up and put on display at the Fort De Soto site.

Private boats visit Egmont Key with regularity – the areas that are open to the public – with visitors exploring the ruins of Fort Dade and enjoying one of the area's most pristine and unspoiled beaches. A ferry from the Fort De Soto dock makes one or two trips over per day, depending on the season.

By contrast, it's estimated that Fort De Soto welcomes between 2 and 3 million people per year. Which is pretty good, considering Henry Fonda, who died in 1982, never came back.

MARILYN MONROE AND JOE DIMAGGIO

3/22/1961 - Redington Beach, FL: Relaxing in a cabana on Redington Beach are Marilyn Monroe and Joe DiMaggio March 22nd. Marilyn is in town for a short vacation while Joe is here with the New York Yankees during their Spring Training acting as their batting coach. Zuma Press/Tampa Bay Times.

Leaning back on a beach recliner under a blue-and-white striped cabana for two, the most-photographed woman in the world smiled shyly at the gathered gaggle of photographers - the newswire paparazzi and the Brownie-toting locals.

"Her skin is white – almost chalky – and her hair is platinum-gold," the daily newspaper would report the next morning. "She's trimmer than the girl in the movies. And she's beautiful. She's really beautiful."

The paper was the *St. Petersburg Times*, and the woman under glass was none other than Marilyn Monroe, actress, sex goddess, living Hollywood legend. Monroe checked into the expansive Tides Hotel in North Redington Beach on March 22, 1961, in the company of her ex-husband, baseball legend Joe DiMaggio.

Although the couple's nine-month marriage had ended acrimoniously six years earlier, they'd remained friendly.

Her latest movie, *The Misfits,* was still in theaters, although the box office receipts were disappointing. The script had been written for Monroe by playwright Arthur Miller, whom she'd wed after her split from DiMaggio. Her divorce from Miller had been finalized in January.

It was, of course, not public knowledge, but the fragile star was well into a downward spiral that included clinical depression, barbiturate abuse and near-constant psychiatric care.

> *"She's trimmer than the girl in the movies. And she's beautiful. She's really beautiful."*

On March 5, she had been discharged from the Neurological Institute at New York's Columbia-Presbyterian Medical Center, following a brief, frightening stay at the Dickensian Payne Whitney Psychiatric Clinic. The ever-protective DiMaggio had threatened to "take the place apart, brick by brick" if Monroe wasn't immediately transferred out of Payne Whitney.

It was DiMaggio who suggested a relaxing week at the beach. The retired Yankee slugger was working as batting coach for the team during spring training in St. Petersburg.

At the Tides, they took separate top-floor suites.

Local residents were allowed limited access to the hotel's two pools, snack bar and beachfront. Membership in the Bath Club wasn't exclusive – anyone who paid the annual dues could use the facility.

"It was all about her – I don't think I even knew who Joe DiMaggio was at the time," says Karen DeYoung, 12 years old in March of 1961. She and her family were Bath Club regulars.

"Everybody was talking about it, as we were hanging out by the pool," she recalls, "so of course we had to go down and check it out. We were giggling and nonchalantly walking in front of their cabana, trying to get a glimpse of them."

DeYoung, senior national security correspondent for the *Washington Post*, has never forgotten what happened next.

"It was at that point that DiMaggio called out 'Hey kid,' and handed me a dollar, or a couple dollars, and said 'Go get us some hot dogs.' So I did."

She ran to the poolside snack bar and dutifully returned, handing a steaming pair of franks to the bare-chested sports icon and the movie star with the chalky-white skin.

They took frequent walks on the beach, holding hands and posing for news photographers. Monroe accompanied her ex to Huggins Field, the Yankees' training site adjacent to Crescent Lake downtown. A photographer from *Sports Illustrated* snapped her gazing adoringly as he swatted a few balls. Together, they watched spring training games from the press box at Al Lang Field.

During their stay, DiMaggio and Monroe dined often in the Tides' on-site restaurant, and at the Wine Cellar, about a mile north on Gulf Boulevard. The Wine Cellar was a favorite haunt for visiting Yankee players.

Mike Porter was 20 years old, a student at St. Petersburg Junior College, working on the valet team at the Wine Cellar. He remembers when the Tides' official "limo," a four-door DeSoto with a wooden rack on the roof, dropped Joe and Marilyn at the restaurant's front door.

"He was sitting in the front seat, she was in back," Porter recalls. "I reached in to help her get out. She was very pale, and very frail. She looked at me and didn't say anything."

They were promptly seated at a dark corner table. "The manager came out about 45 minutes later and said 'Hey, the guests are bothering them so much they can't eat their meal – would you take my car and drive them back to the Tides?'" Porter explains. "I said sure."

Monroe was chatty, Porter remembers, while DiMaggio didn't say much. The two talked about possibly renting a car. They asked him if he had a car of his own.

A day or so later, Porter was summoned to the Tides, poolside, on official business: "I came and picked her up and I took her to get her hair done," he says. "She was delightful; she called me Mike. I didn't make any reference to who she was – I knew she'd had enough of that at the restaurant."

Porter had no interest in Monroe's personal or marital issues. "Other than the fact that she looked great in a bathing suit," he says, "I wasn't into that stuff."

The young student, who lived in a rented cottage on Treasure Island, saw famous people all the time; Yankees star Roger Maris lived across the alley, and he sometimes babysat for the slugger's wife when she went grocery shopping. Micky Mantle was a frequent visitor to the Maris home.

Hotel management arranged for the golden couple to sunbathe in privacy, on a secluded rooftop deck over the lobby. Remembers Bath Club "cabana boy" John Messmore: "They were hounded all the time, so Mr. Dross, the hotel manager, said to them 'Why don't I just give you the key?'"

> *"She ordered an avocado, and an iced tea with two lemons, for lunch."*

Messmore, 17 at the time, was dispatched to the sundeck to take a lunch order. "And when Joe saw me, he thought I was there to get an autograph," Messmore explains. "And that was exactly the opposite of what he wanted. So he wasn't a lot of smiles.

"But Marilyn, I remember she had

Leaving the Tides for dinner at the nearby Wine Cellar restaurant. Zuma Press/Tampa Bay Times.

on a white terrycloth robe, and a kind of white terrycloth wrap thing on her head. And she ordered an avocado, and an iced tea with two lemons, for lunch. And I cannot remember what Joe ordered, I was so enamored with Marilyn Monroe."

Even their secluded rooftop nest wasn't totally private. Boys lined up to throw baseballs to DiMaggio, who'd sign them and toss them back down.

The presence of the famous couple was, naturally, common knowledge to Tides and Bath Club staff. But they were absolutely, positively not to speak to Monroe or DiMaggio unless spoken to, and under no circumstances were they to ask for a photo or an autograph.

On the beach, DiMaggio had snapped, more than once, at locals who got too close to his former wife.

"I do remember her peeking out of the door of her room," Messmore says, "and looking both ways when I was walking down the hallway, like she had heard a noise or something. And that's how I knew which room she was in."

On March 31, the *Times* published a United Press International photo taken the previous afternoon. In another beach cabana, Monroe and DiMaggio were smiling broadly. She was wearing a shoulderless, midriff-bearing top and black shorts.

SUNCOAST SUN GILDS A LILY. Marilyn Monroe arrived on the Suncoast just a week ago today, pale and drawn from a recent illness. Taking her sunglasses off for a cameraman for the first time, Marilyn looks healthy and happy as she poses in a cabana at The Tides, North Redington Beach with her ex-husband, former baseball great, Joe DiMaggio. Both are reported to be leaving the Suncoast area Saturday. Photo: UPI.

On April 1, nine days after their arrival, the couple flew out of Tampa International Airport.

Rumors began to circulate in Hollywood that they were planning to re-marry.

Seventeen months later, Monroe was dead, from an overdose of barbiturates. The coroner ruled her death a possible suicide.

In the interim, she'd started working on a new movie, but was fired from the production after just a few days because of her ongoing health issues, both physical and mental.

The film, ironically, was called *Something's Got to Give.*

BOYD HILL NATURE TRAIL

In the aftermath of 2017's Hurricane Irma, Boyd Hill Nature Preserve Operations Foreman Howard Saytor and his maintenance crew were digging out the root system of an old tree that had blown over.

Their shovels unearthed a collection of bone fragments. And then - a sizeable pair of yellowy-white fangs.

It was, Saytor surmised from the size of the teeth, what remained of Sam, one of two Florida black bears that had lived in a wire-and-concrete cage at the long-ago Boyd Hill Nature Trail zoo.

Sam died in 1976.

"I remember people saying that if some of the animals had passed on after a long, natural life, they actually buried them on the property somewhere," recalled Saytor, who's been with the city-owned preserve in south St. Pete for two decades.

The zoo was located near the entrance of the 245-acre park, on the southern edge of Lake Maggiore (formerly Salt Lake), 380 shallow acres of brackish water. It was named for Boyd Hill, who'd been

Rhesus macaque monkeys at the Boyd Hill Nature Trail zoo, dangerously close to human hands. St. Petersburg Museum of History.

parks superintendent from 1954 until his death from a heart attack in 1957.

Hill's vision for a natural oasis in the middle of a growing city – the term "urban sprawl" wasn't yet in wide usage – was of winding foot paths through pine thickets, sandhill uplands and the marsh and wetlands buffering Lake Maggiore, which had flowed naturally in and out of Tampa Bay until a dam was built in the 1940s.

"The atmosphere of serene peace and quiet is almost tangible," *St. Petersburg Times* columnist Dick Bothwell wrote about Boyd Hill's park in 1958. "And this will be even more priceless an asset in the day when Pinellas is solidly settled, for the original Florida is going fast."

The zoo, however, was noisy. At its peak in the late 1960s, there were an estimated 500 parakeets inside a large wire flight cage (vandals even-

The old zoo: Chain link and concrete. The St. Petersburg Times called it "odoriferous." Boyd Hill Preserve.

tually cut through the wire, and most of the birds escaped into the St. Pete breeze). Monkeys howled. Peacocks roamed the grounds, screaming incessantly.

Admission was just a dime, and so the place was swarming with kids every weekend. Schools made field trips to "Nature Trail" (that's what everyone called it) during the week.

"It was great," remembers Saytor, who was himself a local kid in the 1960s. "Where else were you going to see chimpanzees and bears and stuff? And alligators.

"It was pretty adventurous for the time. There really wasn't that much to do in St. Pete in that era. This was like a little mini-theme park."

Tallahassee attorney George Meros grew up in the neighborhood around Boyd Hill, and fondly remembers it as "just a bike ride away" for him and his siblings.

"It was fun, it was safe, and it was just a great part of growing up in St. Petersburg," Meros says. "Nice people. The most modest of zoos, but plenty of fun for kids our age."

Because the science of animal husbandry was still in its infancy, little thought was given to the captive animals' habitats. Raccoons, deer, alligators, black bears and other indigenous Florida wildlife was caged behind chain-link and chicken-wire alongside non-natives – coata mundi, an ocelot, several species of monkey, an agouti, prairie dogs, the chimps and a pair of South American kinkajous, commonly called "honey bears."

Visitors got used to seeing the animals pacing back and forth in their cramped quarters, all day long, bored and frustrated. The monkeys masturbated and threw feces. Kids learned to dodge.

The menagerie grew over the years; many of the exotic animals were donated to St. Petersburg's sole "zoological park" because their owners just couldn't, or didn't want to, deal with them any longer.

By the mid '70s, Nature Trail zoo was also overrun with penned rabbits and free-roaming ducks and chickens – Easter "gifts" that had grown up and weren't so cute any more – and with prodigiously-breeding guinea pigs.

In 1975, Boyd Hill Nature Trail zoo was cited by the Game and Freshwater Fish Commission for overcrowding, insufficient cage sizes and a number of other violations.

The zoo, it was also noted, was "odoriferous."

Almost everybody hereabouts has oohed and aahed over the animals at Boyd Hill Nature Park zoo. Many a child has had his first real introduction to wildlife there. Lately, though, more and more animal lovers have wandered among the crowded cages with an uneasy feeling that this is a far cry from what nature intended. There's no doubt about it.

St. Petersburg Times editorial/July 21, 1975

The chimpanzees sometimes escaped and caused havoc. Snakes, turtles and other animals were repeatedly stolen. Vandals broke in and clubbed flamingos, rabbits and guinea pigs to death.

The City decided then and there to get out of the roadside attraction business altogether. Noell's Ark Chimp Farm, near Tarpon Springs, bought 100 of the Boyd Hill animals (including 10 goats, four coata mundi and one kinkajou) for $763 in 1977.

Strangely, according to records the "farm" did not take Charlie, the remaining chimpanzee. Charlie's longtime mate, Tammy, had died at Boyd Hill the year before.

After numerous federal animal welfare violations, Noell's Ark was

Sam the black bear in happier times. St. Petersburg Museum of History.

shut down in 1999.

A big-cat breeding facility in Bushnell, Savage Kingdom, purchased the ocelot, an agouti and two foxes. Savage Kingdom was eventually closed by the state government under similar circumstances.

In 1978, the Boyd Hill Nature Park zoo was bulldozed, as part of a massive re-purposing of the property. On (re) opening day, Dec. 14, 1980, Boyd Hill's widow was among the local dignitaries cutting the ribbon on an interpretive nature center, with a fully-stocked library, classrooms, exhibits and laboratories.

The emphasis was now to be on "natural" Florida. However, the team designated by the City to make this transformation happen paved the main trails over with asphalt.

The asphalt was removed after Howard Sayter signed on as foreman. Boyd Hill Nature Preserve - which is operated and maintained by the Department of Parks and Recreation - is his baby, and he has dedicated himself to its future.

"If you lose it," he exclaims, "you lose the biodiversity of what's left. Then you're going to have to go 50, 100 miles away from here to see this. This is a very unique place. I look at Boyd Hill just like a New Yorker would look at Central Park. That's exactly what this is.

> "People don't realize it. This is going to be St. Pete's Central Park."

"People don't realize it. This is going to be St. Pete's Central Park. People still need green space, to go out and walk around, see Florida as what it was before man was here."

A small staff of rangers, biologists and volunteers keep the place running out of the education building (South Branch Library was relocated to Pinellas Point in 2002). There's a fully-licensed raptor rehabilitation center, where Floridian birds of prey deemed unable to fly, or fend for themselves, live out their days inside airy, state-of-the-art flight pens.

It's a far cry from the old zoo, with its primitive, concrete captivity cages.

Because it includes more than six miles of trails through five distinct habitats - hardwood hammocks, sand pine scrub, pine flatwoods, willow marsh and lake shore – Boyd Hill is now one of the most desired hiking destinations in the state. The preserve is also part of the Florida Fish and Wildlife Conservation Commission's Great Florida Birding Trail.

Howard Saytor sees his mission plainly: To erase nearly all of the short-sightedness that went into planning the place back in the 1940s and '50s. To restore the bio-diversity

The popular "old woman in the shoe" slide. Boyd Hill Nature Preserve.

that was lost, or at least plowed over, when man began interfering.

"I'm trying to get the land back to the way it was," he explains. "Boyd Hill introduced a lot of exotic plants out here. It seems to me he was trying to mimic Sunken Gardens. Because Sunken Gardens was really the only thing … and Webb's City, the world's biggest drugstore."

When Saytor arrived, the trails were overgrown. He was stunned to see stocky saw palmettos grown to a height of 12 feet, competing with slash pines and loblolly. Exotics trees and vines were everywhere. "The whole system was out of balance."

So began a dedicated restoration project – to take out, branch by root, all of the exotic, non-Florida plant species, introduce controlled burning, restore the natural water flow from the park to oxygen-starved Lake Maggiore by eliminating storm drain runoff from neighboring streets, and filling in the plethora of purposeless "mosquito ditches" dug by the crews back in Boyd Hill's day.

All of it is a work-in-progress.

Hundreds of plant species that would not normally be found in Florida have become the bane of Howard Saytor's day-to-day life at the park. He can name every one of them, where they came from, what damage they can do. They grow like weeds – which, after all, they are.

"If we want to keep a true representation of Old Florida, we have to remember that invasive species become monocultures – they displace the natural vegetation," Saytor explains. "Which in turn displaces the native wildlife. So it's the complete collapse of a system."

It's an ongoing battle, slashing, burning and ripping out the exotic flora to make conditions optimal for the majestic live oaks, pines, sable palms, red maples, bay, cedar, cypress and sugarberry trees. It's also a horticulturist's dream, to rebuild a healthy world for his beloved plants.

"I'm even trying to bring trees back that historically were here, and had been eradicated," Saytor says proudly.

The ripple effect, since restoration work began, is obvious. Because the decades' accumulation of unchecked undergrowth has been removed through controlled burning – mimicking a natural process – wild hawks, owls and even eagles are making a comeback. The reason? They can now swoop down on prey

A view from the bridge: Lake Maggiore gives way to St. Petersburg's downtown skyline. St. Pete Catalyst.

animals because there's so much more exposed ground.

Likewise, rangers are starting to see more and more newly-hatched gopher tortoises; the vegetarian reptiles' natural food – at ground level - has become much more plentiful since the sunlight reached it.

According to Barbara Stalbird, the City's Natural and Cultural Areas manager, once Boyd Hill's land use designation was changed from "Recreational Open Space" to "Preserve," the chances that the park would ever be sold to developers - local environmentalists' worst nightmare - went from slim to not-at-all.

"Boyd Hill is a charter park, meaning we wouldn't be able to do any kind of use change unless we got a vote from the citizens," she says. "Either way, the park is under extreme protection."

SUNCOAST SEABIRD SANCTUARY

Between 2,500 and 3,000 wild birds arrive at Seaside Seabird Sanctuary every year, some dropped off in cardboard boxes by citizens who've discovered them injured or otherwise incapacitated, others picked up by volunteers on call, trained in the delicate art of handling frightened, feathered creatures in distress.

They all end up at the same 1.5-acre compound in the town of Indian Shores, hard to spot between tall condo buildings on the beach side of Gulf Boulevard.

A majority of the afflicted avians are brown pelicans, synonymous with beach life and boating, with fish hooks piercing their fleshy throats or carelessly cast-off monofilament line wrapped around a leg or a wing and cutting off circulation.

Luckily, says Hospital Director Melissa Dollard, "injury due to fishing line and hooks is very treatable. If they're starving or emaciated, that can complicate their care here. But with pelicans, we have about an 80 percent success rate. Sometimes higher, depending on the time of year."

The worst areas for fishing-relat-

Ralph Heath, mid 1970s. He was Florida's well-known "Bird Man" for decades. State Archives of Florida.

ed pelican injuries, she adds, are the mangrove islands near the Sunshine Skyway Bridge. "Tourists go there to try it, but they don't necessarily know what to do if they hook a bird," Dollard says. "They just cut the line and send that bird on its way."

Pelicans are often found hanging in the mangrove trees, tethered by old fishing line and dying from starvation and exposure.

It's a day-to-day struggle for the seven-member Seaside family and their small army of volunteers.

Even as the sanctuary staffers continue the good work that's been done on their little acre of sand for nearly half a century, there are reminders everywhere of someone whose name is never, ever mentioned.

Ralph Heath Jr. took in sick and injured birds at this very spot on the Gulf coast beginning in the ear-

Hospital Director Melissa Dollard joined the Seaside Seabird Sanctuary team in 2017. Seaside Seabird Sanctuary.

ly 1970s. For decades, his Suncoast Seabird Sanctuary was the largest not-for-profit wild bird sanctuary and rehabilitation center in the United States. More than 50,000 people visited every year, eager for a tour and the hope of a quick chat with Florida's famous "Bird Man."

The boyish, charismatic Heath was one of the best-known residents of Pinellas County. A tireless crusader for wildlife stewardship and conservation, he and the birds in his care were featured in *National Geographic* and the *New York Times*. Charles Kuralt devoted an entire *On the Road* episode to him; he appeared in newspapers and magazines the world over. Heath was feted, awarded and honored. Celebrities came to Florida just to be photographed with him.

In its heyday, Suncoast took in around 45,000 birds annually, from sparrows and blue jays to owls and bald eagles. They'd be brought in with broken wings or legs, or shot, or sick, or starving.

Or worse.

Heath, the son of a doctor, had a University of South Florida degree in pre-med zoology, and with the help of avian veterinarians and a staff just as dedicated to the cause, the birds would be patched up, re-assembled, rehydrated, rehabbed and – when it was time – released back into the wild. Those deemed non-releasable were given permanent homes in the large, open-air pens or roomy flight aviaries on the grounds, which, understandably, became a tourist attraction.

> **The boyish, charismatic Heath was one of the best-known residents of Pinellas County.**

The Suncoast Seabird Sanctuary was a success story like no other. A nonprofit, it had no government pipeline and ran solely on donations. Since Heath owned the beachfront property - it had been his parents' weekend getaway - there was no rent to be paid.

It was idyllic, until it wasn't.

Heath was unceremoniously removed in 2016 following years of legal troubles, including an IRS lien on the property, continuing failure to pay his employees amid accusations of stealing from the sanctuary's donation boxes (a clandestine video showed him doing just that, and stuffing the cash and coins into his pockets). He'd spent $355,000 in sanctuary money on a yacht he referred to as a research vessel, but which was allegedly used mostly for pleasure cruises and parties.

State wildlife officers charged him with 59 misdemeanors in 2014 over the way Suncoast was caring for its feathered residents, and rescinded his permit to treat migratory birds. Staffers and volunteers deserted him.

Most troubling was the evidence procured in a police raid on a windowless Largo warehouse owned by Heath. There, they discovered dozens of birds – some of them missing limbs, some of them blind – wandering the dark facility, and a collection

From left: Dollard, Avian Hospital Specialist Amy Nulph, Director of Operations Keith Wilkins. St. Pete Catalyst.

of turtles in "deplorable" conditions, the floors thick with animal waste and rotting fruit. Heath, then 72, was charged with possessing migratory birds with an expired license, trying to rehabilitate injured wildlife in an unapproved location and possessing box turtles without a permit.

By the time of the raid, Heath had already been kicked out of 18328 Gulf Boulevard. He'd sold the family home, in 2011, to a Dallas-based company called Seaside Land Investments, LLC, which removed him, and the entity known as Suncoast Seabird Sanctuary. They even changed the locks.

Three of the principals in Seaside Land Investments are Heath's sons, Andrew, Alex and Peter von Gontard, from his five-year marriage to beer heiress Beatrice Busch in the 1980s. The boys eventually took the surname of their stepfather, Adel von Gontard. And together they set out to rehabilitate what was left of Pinellas County's legendary bird sanctuary and its tattered reputation.

Andrew, Alex and their stepfather sit on the board of Seaside Seabird Sanctuary (Andrew is the president). They all reside out of state.

Seaside Seabird Sanctuary Director of Operations Keith Wilkins is quick to point out that Seaside is an entirely different entity, and has no tether whatsoever to Ralph Heath's Suncoast.

There's a large open-air rehab area hidden from public view – the state and federal Fish and Wildlife Conservation Commissions insist on that – and a walkable public section with 100 or so permanent, non-releasable residents.

As in Heath's day, the sanctuary operates entirely on public donations.

The laws governing the care and captivity of wild birds, however, have grown more restrictive.

In 1975, a pair of crippled brown pelicans hatched a chick at the Suncoast Seabird Sanctuary - the first such event in history. The bird was, at that time, on the Endangered Species List. Over the decades, nearly 200 pelicans were hatched and fledged at Suncoast, and released into the wild, by Heath and his staff, when they were old enough to fend for themselves.

Wild pelicans even built their nests on the sanctuary site, on the very netting that was installed to keep them out of the captive pens. Birds of a feather and all that.

The brown pelican is no longer classified as endangered.

These days, Wilkins explains, "FWC does not allow birds in captivity to mate. We have two different pelican pens, one for the males and one for the females. Even though these are permanently disabled birds, any

> *Seaside is an entirely different entity, and has no tether whatsoever to Ralph Heath's Suncoast.*

offspring they had would potentially be healthy. And we're not legally allowed to hold onto a healthy bird, and put it on display to the public. It has to be released.

> **The laws governing the care and captivity of wild birds have grown more restrictive.**

"We can't immediately release a captive-hatched pelican; it needs to be raised by its parents to learn how to survive out in the wild. And even if FWC said well, OK, there's an accident and you have two birds that mate, you're allowed to keep it until it's raised by the parents ... the thing is, the parents can't raise their young on how to properly survive in the wild in captivity."

Wilkins, a Michigan native who worked for many years as a Florida concert promoter, started as a volunteer at Suncoast, shortly before Heath was unceremoniously asked to leave.

Only a few of Heath's volunteers remain from those dark last days.

Although Wilkins is often asked to speak to local civic groups and wildlife organizations, he has little to no interest in becoming a celebrity spokesperson.

"Our main reason for being here is to rehabilitate birds," he says squarely. "If we had to give up one or the other, it would be the attraction aspect. We would be here just to rescue, treat and rehabilitate birds."

While the Seaside hospital director makes the determination that a disabled pelican, gull or wading bird can enjoy a good quality of life in captivity, FWC has the final say.

Fish and Wildlife reviews all of the sanctuary's paperwork – "We have to report everything, like all rehabbers do," Wilkins says - and periodic inspections double-check the facility itself.

Ralph Heath's father, a prominent Tampa surgeon, bought the beach house in the 1950s for family weekends (the home itself is technically over the line in Redington Shores). When he was a kid, Heath used to say, theirs was one of the only buildings on the beach. You could look for a quarter mile, north or south, and not see another sign of human activity.

Over the years, he watched as the little concrete block home – and the bird rehab center he built on the north side of his dad's lot – was dwarfed, one high rise at a time, until the beach itself wasn't even visible from nearby Gulf Boulevard.

In a 2010 interview with WMNF's *Talking Animals,* Heath described the sanctuary's humble beginnings. In 1971, he explained, "I had decided to be a well-educated beach bum. After about a seven-year college education, I said 'I'm going to collect driftwood and make lamps.'"

On a December morning, he remembered, he came across a cormorant by the side of Gulf Boulevard, dragging a badly broken wing. "My father had helped me take care of birds and animals and reptiles that were hurt over the years, because he was such an incredible surgeon," Heath said. "But he was in Tampa."

So Heath contacted a veterinarian he knew in western St. Petersburg. The doctor surgically repaired the wing with a steel pin, sewed things up, and the little seabird was on its way to mending.

"I've done my job," he told Ralph Heath. "Now it's up to you."

ENTERTAINMENT & FUN

THE MANHATTAN CASINO

GRAND FORKS, N.D. – Trumpet player Louis (Satchmo) Armstrong said yesterday he's given up plans for a government-sponsored trip to Russia because "The way they are treating my people in the South, the government can go to hell ... it's getting almost so bad, a colored man hasn't got any country."

Associated Press/Sept. 19, 1957

Louis Armstrong was on one wild ride in 1957. Arguably the best-known jazz musician in America, he was playing to packed houses, and in the Jim Crow South – where the audiences were almost always segregated – he'd endured death threats, and bomb threats, and one day in January several sticks of dynamite exploded outside a Knoxville auditorium while he was onstage with his combo. No one was injured, and Armstrong kept the 3,000-strong

Feb. 28, 1957: Louis Armstrong (center) and band perform to a packed, largely unsegregated house at the Manhattan Casino. Tampa Bay Times/Zuma Press.

The gospel-singing Soul Stirrers debuted at the Manhattan Casino in 1950, and returned for several years until lead singer Sam Cooke (lower left) departed for a secular solo career.

Ray Charles

playing the so-called Chitlin' Circuit, a loosely-connected network of Black nightclubs and tiny performance venues in the South. African American entertainers found steady work on the circuit, pulling one-nighters in embattled, segregated times. He had long since graduated to the "big leagues."

In February 1957, a few weeks after the explosion in Tennessee, Armstrong brought his band to the Manhattan Casino, a 6,000-square foot dancing hall on St. Petersburg's South Side. The Manhattan was a

crowd's spirit up by quipping "That sounded like a drunk falling out of the balcony." And then he played another tune.

But the whole lamentable situation bugged him.

White, middle class America had the affable trumpeter in its focus because of his co-starring appearance alongside Frank Sinatra, Bing Crosby and Grace Kelly in *High Society*, one of the biggest box office hits of 1956. He was selling records by the millions. He played Carnegie Hall. He toured the world. The U.S. State Department crowned him its International Jazz Ambassador.

But Armstrong made his bones

Dancing the night away. Photo courtesy of Paul Barco/St. Petersburg Museum of History.

regular stop on the Chitlin' Circuit, and hundreds of performing musicians appeared there between the post-Depression '30s and 1968, when it closed for good.

He'd performed there twice in the 1940s. By 1957, Louis Armstrong was, arguably, too big to play a gig at the Manhattan Casino, which could barely hold 500 people. But he did it anyway. The small, sold-out audience was half Black and half white.

Backstage, a *St. Petersburg Times* reporter asked his opinion on segregation. "I don't bother about those fellows," Armstrong replied with his trademark grin. "I just blow my horn."

For 25 years – between 1939 and 1964 – the Manhattan Casino was where Black artists, whether they played jazz, blues, swing, rhythm 'n' blues, rock 'n' roll or something between the cracks, could always find a sympathetic crowd. A welcoming audience, grateful for the entertainment and the fellowship, where it wasn't likely there'd be somebody trying to use dynamite to scare, intimidate or wipe them from the face of the earth.

B.B. King

Many of the greatest names in music – Black or otherwise – "just blew their horns" at the Manhattan: Ella Fitzgerald, Count Basie, James Brown, B.B. King, Ray Charles, Etta James, Otis Redding, Dinah Washington, Sam Cooke, Little Richard, Bo Diddley, the Coasters, Jimmy Reed, Sister Rosetta Tharpe … it is a more-than-impressive list (see be-

House band, date unknown: From left: Fess Clark, Al Williams, George Brown, Warren Rainey and Leroy Barton. St. Petersburg Museum of History, from the Al Williams Collection.

low).

For years I played night clubs, working the Chitlin' Circuit. These clubs were very small, very tight, very crowded and very loud. Everything was loud but the entertainment. The only way to establish communication was by telling a story that would lead into the song, that would catch people's attention.

Lou Rawls/Los Angeles Times, Jan. 8, 1967

Built in 1926 by pioneering St. Pete developer Elder Jordan, the Manhattan was conceived as a community center for the historically Black neighborhood known as The Deuces, where 22nd Street South meets 22nd Avenue South.

The dance hall occupied the entire second floor of Jordan's 12,000-square-foot building. It was a spacious open room, with a stage three feet off the ground, a polished hardwood dance floor and wooden benches against the opposite walls.

Here, Gibbs High School – which did not have an auditorium or meeting space of its own until the mid 1940s – held its proms, sock hops and graduation ceremonies. Church socials took place there. There were beauty pageants and "baby shows." Ladies' teas and fashion parades. The Manhattan was where people came together for social gatherings, meetings, holiday parties and celebrations … and regularly scheduled dances.

"Twenty-second," recalls Ron Gregg, 74, "was like Broadway in New York for African Americans here. Because it was the only place we could go for entertainment."

Sundays were reserved for gospel performances. Goldie Thompson, disc jockey for a Tampa religious station and an ambitious, smooth-talking promoter, brought in singing groups from around the country for good-natured "competitions."

In the 1940s and '50s, when Thompson's gospel shows were at their zenith, the touring groups included, among others, The Dixie Hummingbirds, The Five Blind Boys of Alabama (later known as The Happyland Singers), The Fairfield Four, The Five Blind Boys of Jackson, Miss., The Kings of Harmony, The Reliable Jubilee Singers, The Swan Silvertone Singers, The Skylarks of Nashville, The Spirit of Memphis and the CBC Trumpeteers.

On March 19, 1950 the Soul Stirrers, from Chicago, made their Manhattan Casino debut. The group's lead singer, new that year, was 19-year-old Sam Cooke. The Soul Stirrers made annual appearances until 1956, when Cooke departed for a solo career.

The "national" popular music shows began in 1939, with the St. Pete debut of 22-year-old Ella Fitzgerald and her band.

The casino – which, pointedly, was not a gambling establishment and did not sell alcohol – was often jammed. Those too young to get in, or who couldn't afford the admission, sat and stood in the parking lot across the street, listening to the music coming through the upstairs jalousie windows. Many listened from their cars.

Most weekends, and other nights that offered the opportunity for dancing, promoter George Grogan put local jazz and swing groups onstage, including A.C. Jones and the Atomic Aces, and – in the '60s – Al

Nov. 26, 1956: Little Richard (center) and band at the Manhattan Casino. Photo courtesy Minson R. Rubin/ St. Petersburg Museum of History.

Williams & the Versatiles.

Grogan taught chemistry at Gibbs High, and managed the Jordan Park neighborhood (named for Elder Jordan, who built the Manhattan Casino). He also had connections in the New York talent agencies. "We plan to bring the best possible entertainment throughout the year," Grogan told the *Times* in 1956. "By visiting booking offices personally in early October, we're able to get dates before the best ones are taken. People here prefer Friday night dances, and as nearly as possible we're going to give them those play dates."

The Manzy Harris Orchestra (from Tampa) and Buddy Johnson Orchestra (from New York) were frequent guests, as well. Pre-World War II, the house band was Fess Clark and His Swingsters; St. Petersburg's George Cooper and orchestra later had the honors, gigging regularly every Monday night.

Depending on the visiting artist,

Etta James

these groups would back the headliners during their shows, and play dance music during intermission.

(Manzy Harris was an important figure in the life and career of Ray Charles, who performed at the Manhattan numerous times in the 1950s.)

Because "white" hotels in the city refused to rent rooms to Blacks, Grogan and the other promoters arranged for the performers to bunk in rooming houses near The Deuces, or in private homes; some families were only too glad to help out.

"That was the only places musicians could stay," says Ron Gregg, a jazz drummer who's heard all the stories, many of them firsthand.

Gregg was a youngster during the mid-50s heyday of the Manhattan Casino, but he has very vivid memories of his own: "I would see the musicians' buses roll in. They would come into town, and a lot of them would have their jackets over their arms, wearing white shirts, and their black bow ties attached to their collars. Walking up and down the street, trying to find someplace to eat and relax until they had to play that night. And I said to myself 'They must be musicians.'"

The morning after the show, the

> **The dance hall occupied the entire second floor of Elder Jordan's 12,000-square-foot building.**

musicians – well-rested and (ideally) well-fed – would load up their instruments, climb back into the bus, or whatever cars they'd come in, and head for the next stop on the circuit – Tampa, most likely, or Gainesville. Or Jacksonville.

Time – the way it will – did a number on the Manhattan. The very last "major" concert, in 1964, starred B.B. King, who'd been a consistent draw there since the early '50s. The Civil Rights Act made sweeping changes in the way people of color were treated in the United States, and although it wasn't a smooth transition (particularly in the South), the Chitlin' Circuit itself faded into memory.

By 1968, the Casino was well past its prime, as other venues, most with air conditioning, drew paying customers away from what was, admittedly, a neighborhood in decline. With little fanfare, it closed, and remained that way for 18 years. St. Petersburg's city council gave it historic landmark designation in 1994, and the two-story building – 12,000 square feet in total – was purchased by the City in 2002.

Now known as The Historic Manhattan Casino, the dance hall has been extensively remodeled, and at this writing is in transition yet again – the City recently approved a new concept by its lessee, the Callaloo Restaurant Group, for an expanded "food hall" with several dining options, along with a small-business incubator operated by Rising Tide Innovation Center.

The Manhattan Casino, and the Deuces neighborhood, are part of the city's South St. Petersburg Community Redevelopment Area. There continue to be heated discussions, both privately and in public, about just what constitutes "restoration" and "revitalization."

But if those walls could talk ...

Otis Redding

The shows

What follows is a curated list of the national, touring performers – the legends of blues, jazz and soul music– who appeared onstage at the Manhattan Casino between 1939 and 1964. The list was compiled from the archives of the St. Petersburg Times: stories, show listings and advertisements. The list is by no means complete; it does not include local concerts, dances or other social events, not does it include the many, many gospel shows produced by Goldie Thompson.

Note: A local legend persists that

Duke Ellington was among the music icons who performed at the Manhattan Casino. While it is documented that Ellington and orchestra performed at the (very white) St. Petersburg Coliseum on three occasions – in 1937 (during his very first Florida swing), 1955 and 1956, there is no record of a stop at the Manhattan. The website dukeellington.org.uk includes an obsessive day-by-day accounting of Ellington's touring schedule, and a Manhattan date does not appear anywhere in the archives (listings or advertisements) of the *Times*.

1939. Ella Fitzgerald

1940. Ink Spots, Fats Waller, Coleman Hawkins, Louis Armstrong

1941. International Sweethearts of Rhythm (all-girl orchestra)

1943. Lil Green & Tiny Bradshaw, Barney Johnson Orchestra and Brown Skin Models

1944. Snookum Russell & His Orchestra, Eddie Durham's All-Girl Orchestra, Marva Louis (singing wife of prizefighter Joe Louis), with Nat Towles and His Orchestra, Lil Green, Delta River Boys, Luis Russell, Erskine Hawkins & His Tuxedo Junction Orchestra, Lucky Millinder (featuring Judy Carroll and Trevor Bacon) with Wynonie Harris, Cootie Williams and Eddie Vinson

1945: International Sweethearts of Rhythm (all-girl orchestra), Oran "Hot Lips" Page & His Orchestra, Louis Jordan and His Tympani Five; Fletcher Henderson, Sister Rosetta Tharpe with Lucky Millinder (featuring Judy Carroll and Trevor Bacon) and Wynonie Harris

1946. Erskine Hawkins & His Tuxedo Junction Orchestra, Louis Armstrong, Eddie "Cleanhead" Vinson, Joe Liggins & His Honeydrippers Orchestra

1947: Jimmie Lunceford & His Orchestra, Charlie Brontley and His Honey Dippers Orchestra

1948: Golden Gate Quartette, Erskine Hawkins & His Tuxedo Junction Orchestra Featuring Jimmy Mitchell, Jimmie Lunceford Orchestra with

Sister Rosetta Tharpe

Joe Thomas and Eddie Wilcox, Lonnie Johnson, Ella Johnson and Arthur Prysock with the Buddy Johnson Orchestra, Louis Jordan & His Tympani Five, Vi Burnside & the International Sweethearts of Rhythm

1949. Sister Rosetta Tharpe and Marie Knight, Roy Brown, Chubby Newsom, Joe Liggins & His Honeydrippers Orchestra, Bullmoose Jackson and His Buffalo Bearcats, Marie Knight with Vivian Cooper

1950. Marie Knight with Vivian Cooper, Sister Rosetta Tharpe, Soul Stirrers

1951. "Battle of the Saxaphones" (sic) with Bullmoose Jackson and Frank Cully, Bullmoose Jackson and His Buffalo Bearcats, Cab Calloway (this band included Cozy Cole, Chu Berry and Dizzy Gillespie), Dinah Washington, Earl Bostic

1952. Eddie "Cleanhead" Vinson, Johnny Otis Orchestra with Little Esther, Mel Walker & Red Lyte, Erskine Hawkins, Marie Knight, Wynonie Harris, Larry Darnell, Arthur Prysock, Peppermint Harris, Joan Shaw & Veretta Dillard, Earl Bostic

1953. Johnny Otis with Willie Mae (Big Mama) Thornton & Sally Blair, Clarence Gatemouth Brown, Tiny Bradshaw and His Jersey Bounce Orchestra, Johnny Ace with Willie Mae (Big Mama) Thornton, B.B. King (twice this year).

1954. Charles Brown and Lowell Fulson, Dinah Washington, Cootie Williams & the Checkers, Tiny Bradshaw and His Jersey Bounce Orchestra

1955. Roy Milton, Chuck Willis, Bo Diddley and Jimmy Witherspoon, Drifters (with Walking Willie & His Swinging Bluesmen, tap dancers

Aretha Franklin

Count Basie

Bo Diddley

Moore and Moore, trumpeter Irving Johnson and "the sexotic dancing of Vida DuSoir"), Pee Wee Crayton, B. B. King, The Midnighters (with lead vocalist Hank Ballard, who would write "The Twist" in 1959), Charles Brown

1956. B.B. King, Lloyd Price, Big Joe Turner, Drifters, Willis Jackson and Little Willie John, Clifton Chernier & the Playboys, Ray Charles, Guitar Slim and Lloyd Lambert, Ruth Brown, Ann Cole and Muddy Waters, LaVern Baker, Little Richard, Flames Quintet (with James Brown), Chuck Willis, Midnighters

1957. 5 Royales, Louis Armstrong, Erskine Hawkins, Louis Jordan, Lloyd Price, Little Willie John, Etta James with Huey P. Smith and Buddy Griffin, Big Joe Turner, Robust Roy Brown, Willie Dixon and Otis Rush, Ann Cole & Jimmy Rogers, Bill Doggett, Ray Charles, Shirley and Lee, Wynonie Harris, Big Maybelle, Little Willie John, Noble "Thin Man" Watts, Lloyd Price, Joe Tex, Marie Knight & The Ravens, Ruth Brown

1958. Drifters (most likely the post-Clyde McPhatter, pre-Ben E. King Drifters), Bill Doggett, Erskine Hawkins, Ray Charles, Silhouettes, Gene Allison, Lloyd Price, Big Joe Turner, James Brown & His Famous Flames, Shirley and Lee and Fats Domino, Jimmy Reed, Little Willie John, Ruth Brown, Ray Charles, B.B. King, The Pastels

1959. Jimmy Reed, Ray Charles, Dizzy Gillespie, The Coasters, Staple Singers, Amos Milburn & Charles Brown, Paul Williams and Ruth Brown, Jimmy Reed

1960. Drifters (three times this year), Ruth Brown

1961. Dee Clark, Bill Doggett, Ruth Brown, Jimmy Smith, Little Willie John

1962. B.B. King, Count Basie Orchestra (according to the *Times* review, 1,000 people attended), Texas Ray & the Gene Franklin Orchestra, Bill Doggett, 5 Royales, Bobby "Blue" Bland, Bobby Williams & His Orchestra with featured vocalists Little Tammie John and Aretha Franklin, Jimmy Smith

1963. Maxine Brown, Jerry Butler (canceled, as Butler was injured in a car crash while touring in Florida), Otis Redding/Carla Thomas/Booker T & the MGs, B.B. King (twice), Big Joe Henderson, Little Johnny Taylor, Bobby "Blue" Bland

1964. B.B. King

Erik Rhodes and Ronnie Cunningham in "The Firefly," 1951. All photos in this chapter by Phil Graham.

THE OPERETTA AND THE MUSIC CIRCUS

When professional musical theater made its grand entrance in St. Petersburg, it wasn't with major-league stars, first class sound and lights and Broadway-style creature comforts like air conditioning and cushioned seats.

In January, 1951, what St. Petersburg got was a canvas, big top-style tent in a vacant lot, with a 43-foot ceiling and 1,400 hard wooden chairs set on staggered platforms directed at the circular stage, at ground level in the center of the tent.

Still, the arrival of the St. Petersburg Operetta was big news; the actors, actresses, singers and dancers were stage veterans, from New York and around the country, and the productions themselves – light musicals like *The Student Prince, The Vagabond King* and *Naughty Marietta* – were well-tuned crowd-pleasers and performed with a live orchestra (set in a pit dug lower than the floor).

Since nothing much ever happened in St. Petersburg, the local papers treated the Operetta debut like a visit from the Royal Family.

The venture's P.T. Barnum-like central character was Pennsylvanian public relations man, short story writer and wannabe impresario Pat Hurley, who convinced four Philadelphia businessmen to invest $50,000 each to fund the St. Petersburg Operetta. Drugstore magnate William Sylk had two sons enrolled at Admiral Farragut Academy here. Financier Jay Cooke had been stationed in Florida during World War II (he had also unsuccessfully run for governor of Pennsylvania, with Hurley as his campaign manager).

The idea – and it seemed like a darn good one – was to bring the professionals to Florida for 13 weeks in the winter. A variation on summer stock - a repertory company that would stay in the same place for a while, performing a rotating season of shows.

Bring some culture to the hicks in the sticks. And stay warm in the bargain!

Hurley had a real horse in the race in his business partner Wilbur Evans, a theater and radio veteran with a booming baritone voice and a dashing, likable-rascal stage persona. Evans would star in most of each season's 12 planned shows, and direct them all.

Soprano and "prima donna" Victoria Sherry's husband Roland Fiore – a talented composer and conductor from New York City Center Opera - was hired as Musical Director.

Tented theater-in-the-round was something of a national craze at the time. The style was pioneered by showman St. John (aka Sinjin) Terrell in post-war New Jersey; his Lambertville Music Circus was an immediate success and spawned copycats across the country.

Terrell himself was busy spreading his brand; in 1950 he opened a Music Circus in Miami, and for reasons unknown chose tiny, undeveloped

In "The Merry Widow," clockwise from left Sherry, Rotov, MacCaulay and Burris.

Clockwise from top left, head shots for Doris McKee and Jack Goode; Ruth Webb and John MaCaulay (both in costume for "The Vagabond King").

Treasure Island as the company's "sister" city.

One of Terrell's business partners was producer Robert Aldrich, husband of British stage star Gertrude Lawrence. She and Aldrich were part owners of a Terrell tent stage in Hyannis, Massachusetts.

Hurley and Terrell must have kept tabs on one another, although there's no record of either of them complaining about – or even mentioning - the competition.

> **The destruction of the tent was just one factor in Hurley's decision to move the Operetta into a permanent location.**

Located in a circus tent at the intersection of Gulf Boulevard and the Treasure Island Causeway, the Treasure Island Music Circus debuted Jan. 9, 1951 with *Song of Norway*.

Six days later and 18 miles away, the St. Petersburg Operetta opened its first production, *The Merry Widow*. The battle for theatrical supremacy was on.

In the end, it wasn't much of a battle. Attendance was low out at the T.I. tent – halfway through the second week's show, *No No Nanette*, the decision was made to pull the plug and send the company back to Miami (among the cast was a young "hopeful" named Elaine Stritch; the teenaged assistant stage director was Larry Hagman, son of actual Broadway icon Mary Martin, and the future *I Dream of Jeannie* and *Dallas* TV star).

After *Carousel* took its final bows Jan. 28, the Treasure Island Music Circus folded its tent.

"This is just not the place for us," manager Arthur Gerold told the *St. Petersburg Times*. "Our productions are very high class and expensive ... if we lowered the quality, it would not be the Music Circus. Your town does not seem to be able to afford this type of entertainment, judging from our audiences, and it would not pay us to continue."

Sherry had the lead role in the Operetta production of *The Merry Widow*, with Evans – who also directed – as her leading man. The cast also included handsome tenor Glenn Burris, towering character actor Joseph MacCauley and 4-foot-9 "satirical" dancer Alex Ritov. "Rotov is so tiny the children who pack matinees adore him as an animated Charlie McCarthy," howled the *Times*. "And their parents shriek with laughter at his ballet satires."

These five would be the core of the Operetta company for its first 13-week season, although others would come and go as needed.

Theatre-in-the-round is much more demanding than Broadway shows. I was in Up in Central Park *for 22 months - it was nothing compared to this. While we're doing one show, we're learning another. Thus a lead must learn five or six songs, 35-40 pages of dialogue per week. So that a principal has perhaps 10 different songs buzzing around in his head, to say nothing of 80 or 90 lines.*

Wilbur Evans/St. Petersburg Times, March 25, 1951

Week after week, it was a cold winter. "The modern thermostatic oil heating plant keeps the canvas operadome at comfortable levels," declared the *Times*, but playgoers complained anyway about the chills, and about the uncomfortable seats, and about the difficulty in understanding the dialogue from the faraway circular stage.

On April 2, with just two performances left for *The Great Waltz*, the final show of the year, high winds blew the Operetta tent over. Evans, Sherry, McCaulay and the rest of the cast ended their inaugural season onstage in the St. Petersburg High School auditorium.

The destruction of the tent was just one factor in Hurley's decision to move the Operetta into a permanent location, with real walls and a real roof and not so far from downtown. A race track, Tri-City Speedway, had been proposed for the neighborhood. Loud, constant noise was something the Operetta most definitely did not need.

He brokered a deal with the owners of Gay Blades Roller Rink, 2191 9th Avenue North, to house the next five Operetta seasons there. The price tag for a 13-week lease of the pseudo-Quonset Hut was $15,000.

(This was before Gay Blades was taken over by the Gould family, who made a three-decade success out of the recreation facility.)

The second season began on Jan. 2, 1952, with the (non-air conditioned)

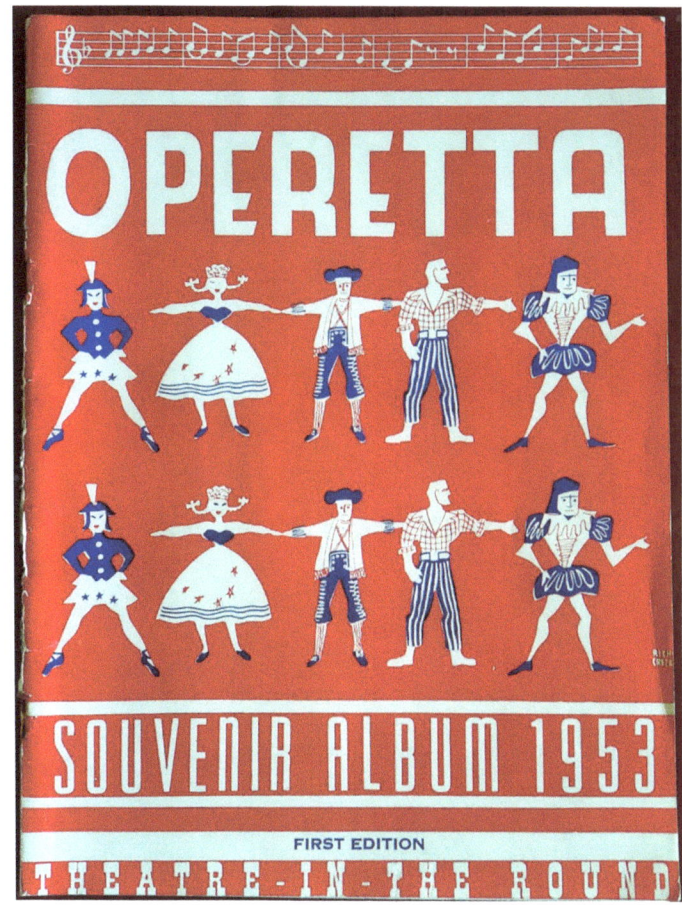

roller rink temporarily fitted out with a central stage and the same angled wooden platforms and rows of seats. The capacity, again, was 1,400.

Missing in action was perennial leading man Wilbur Evans, who'd opened in the fall in *South Pacific*, opposite Mary Martin, on London's West End. Evans never returned to St. Petersburg.

The cast of financial backers changed, too, as Hurley's First Four stayed home in Pennsylvania. The new money men – all local - included contractor W.C. Gorman and realtor D.D. Rosselli.

The business became The Operetta Corporation, and the investors announced an intention to make money, rather than lose it as Hurley had done in his "tent season."

Victoria Sherry remained as the company's main female lead, with husband Fiore staying aboard as well. The shows included *Brigadoon, Carousel, Sally, The Merry Widow* (again), *The Red Mill* and similarly frothy fare.

In March, Hurley boasted to a reporter that the Operetta was operating squarely in the black, and that plans were being finalized to open a second location in Tampa, rotating the same shows and casts. He also said he was negotiating to bring the enterprise to Orlando, Jacksonville, Atlanta and New Orleans.

None of which ever happened.

Hurley reported outstanding attendance figures for each of the shows, averaging more than 10,000 guests for each production's seven-week run in the made-over roller palace.

When Season Three began in January, 1953, only Sherry, Fiore and dancer Rotov remained from the original company.

Stephen Douglass, who'd played Billy Bigelow in the Broadway pro-

In the tent: MacCaulay, Rhodes and Rosemarie Brancato in "The Firefly," 1951.

duction of *Carousel*, and launched the role in the West End, assayed it again for the Operetta's season-opener. Others performing in Season Three included Joan Kibrig, Van Hawley (who would go on to co-star in the horror film *The Monster*), John Shanks, Colee Worth, Hawaiian singer/actor Dick Smart, Margaret Irving, Earle MacVeigh and (returning from the second season) Rosemarie Brancato and Stanley Carlson.

Choreographer Jamie Jamieson, who arranged the hotfoot hoofing for *The Wizard of Oz, Kiss Me Kate, High Button Shoes* and the rest of the third season's crowd-pleasers, later went on to work with Agnes DeMille on numerous revivals of *Brigadoon*, and became one of the best-known Scottish Highland performers in the dance world.

The plot thickened considerably in February when the Board of Directors voted to fire Hurley, catching the Operetta's founder and producer – so he claimed – completely by surprise.

Gorman and Rosselli said that they and the other directors felt that Hurley had not given his best to the Operetta and that it was that they believed he had not fulfilled his duties that his contract had been abrogated ... "We are parting with Hurley for what we hope are for the best interests of the community," Gorman said. "We want to do everything we can for this city."

St. Petersburg Times, Feb. 13, 1953

From there, the end came swiftly. On May 10, it was announced that The Operetta Corporation and the owners of Gay Blades Roller Rink could not reach an agreement on a lease extension. Gay Blades co-owner Bill Bryan offered to host a 1954 season for a reduced rate of $12,000; Gorman and company suggested $8,000, and a small percentage of the profits.

And Bryan told them to stuff it.

Ticket sales for a post-Hurley fourth

> **Ticket sales began for a fourth season, but the bottom fell out and it never happened.**

season began in the summer, although the shows had not been fi-

A publicity shot for "The Vagabond King," with Wilbur Evans and Victoria Sherry.

nalized and a new location had yet to be secured.

An aircraft hangar at Albert Whitted Field was considered, but ruled out, as was another big-top tent south of downtown. Both St. Petersburg Junior College and Boca Ciega High School turned down auditorium lease requests.

In late January, refunds were mailed in the form of checks signed by Operetta President Donald Rosselli. An accompanying letter read, in part: "Being unable to secure a site, the producer was forced to abandon his plan for 1954. The chances are excellent that an operetta season will be held in 1955."

Rosselli said he had "no idea" how many checks had been issued but explained he had signed a "slew." He said he had "no comment whatsoever" to make in connection with the refunds or announcement of the Operetta failure.

St. Petersburg Times, January 26, 1954

And with that last scene, the curtain fell on Act One of professional musical theater in St. Petersburg.

Musical director Roland Fiore, left, and director Wilbur Evans watch Evans' wife, film actress Susanna Foster, perfect a dance move.

The Operetta's second home, the Gay Blades Roller Rink Quonset Hut.

THE BAYFRONT CENTER

The Mahaffey Theater has been part of the downtown St. Petersburg landscape since 1965, although it's changed considerably in appearance and stature.

For 22 years, it was a boxy little part of the city's ambitious ($5 million, in early '60s money) Bayfront Center complex, attached at the hip to a 7,000-seat arena where families gathered to see Holiday on Ice, the Lipizzaner Stallions and the Ringling Brothers/Barnum & Bailey Circus, where sports fans cheered on soccer's Tampa Bay Rowdies, and the Suncoast Suns ice hockey team, and where - later on - the likes of Bruce Springsteen, Van Halen, Elton John and the Grateful Dead attracted massive amounts of enthusiastic fans.

All the big "adult" spectacle acts – Elvis, Liberace, Lawrence Welk and TV-era Sonny & Cher - performed in the big hall, too, which everyone referred to as simply the Bayfront Center.

The Bayfront Theater, as the Mahaffey was known, was reserved for smaller crowds (the original venue had slightly fewer than 2,000 seats)

Postcard image.

and more "sophisticated" entertainment like orchestras, operas and ballets.

In the early years the theater was programmed almost exclusively for St. Petersburg's older population – easy listening acts such as Ferrante and Teicher, Sandler & Young, Peter Nero and Roger Williams made annual appearances.

Louis Armstrong, who in previous years had performed at both the Manhattan Casino and the St. Petersburg Coliseum, headlined at the Bayfront Theater in December, 1966.

The City was slow to put popular music acts on the stage. The first "rock groups" to play the theater were the Turtles and Bubble Puppy in March, 1969 – nearly four years after the place had opened.

By the mid 1970s, "soft" artists along the lines of Gordon Lightfoot, Melissa Manchester, George Benson and Chuck Mangione were infiltrating the lineup, interspersed between the bread and butter acts – the Fred Waring Orchestra, the Lettermen, Johnny Mathis, the Vienna Boys Choir – and septuagenarian Victor Borge, whose cornball comedy mixed with classical piano-playing was such a hit with the St. Pete oldsters the Bayfront Theater was on his touring itinerary every year for decades.

Because the Bayfront Center was city-owned, the two venues were also booked for high school graduations, business conventions, political rallies and other civic events. (Richard Nixon famously spoke to a packed arena in October, 1970, the first time a sitting U.S. president had ever visited Pinellas County.)

The major rock artists began to make regular stops at the arena - mega-acts of the mid to late '70s including Jethro Tull, Tom Petty & the Heartbreakers, Jimmy Buffett, the Police, Rush, Cheap Trick and Journey.

Things began to change in the 1980s. Competition for those big touring dollars meant newer, more state-of-the-art venues like the USF Sun Dome in Tampa and the Lakeland Civic Center began to tear away at the Bayfront arena's business.

The little theater, on the other hand, had fans with deeper pockets.

In 1987, St. Petersburg's Mahaffey family spearheaded a $24.5 million renovation of the Bayfront Theater, which had become seriously outdated. Among other significant physical changes, "window box" seats were built, to give the newly-plush venue the appearance of a European opera house. The name was officially changed.

By 2004, the aging arena next door

> **The major rock artists began to make regular stops at the arena in the 1970s.**

was hemorrhaging money, and the City decided to tear it down. The Mahaffey Theater was left standing on its own, the anchor property on big, open and otherwise vacant waterfront acreage.

Things went well for the Mahaffey for a few years, until poor programming choices and the waning interest of the public delivered yet an-

Frequent visitor Lawrence Welk helps Bayfront manager Al Legatt celebrate the arena's first decade, 1975. City of St. Petersburg.

other showdown. It was either admit defeat and shut it down, or try to bring it into the future.

In 2011, businessman Bill Edwards was granted a contract to manage the facility through his Big3 Entertainment. Edwards also kicked in for upgrades and expansion of the lobby – today, you'd never know it was once bolted to an ice-skating arena – and the construction of the trademark glass atrium windows.

That same year, the new City-owned Salvador Dali Museum building opened, across the grass courtyard from the Mahaffey (today, the

College basketball in the arena (USF vs. FSU), 1970s. City of St. Petersburg.

The Ringling Brothers Barnum & Bailey Circus was a regular visitor; the Bayfront performances were filmed for the circus' annual TV special. City of St. Petersburg.

museum, and the courtyard, rest on the former site of the Bayfront arena).

The city has extended Big3's management contract several times, as more high-end shows - from the likes of Jerry Seinfeld, Tony Bennett, Diana Ross, Steve Martin and others - and a growing reputation for both quality and luxury have generated profits and positive word-of-mouth.

It became the Duke Energy Center for the Arts Mahaffey Theater in 2013.

Making history

The Bayfront Center was officially dedicated on May 6, 1965. Comedian Jonathan Winters emceed a glitzy gala, co-starring singer Nancy Ames, the Highwaymen and a TV-style orchestra.

The *St. Petersburg Times* covered the event with three next-day stories. "Both the young and old attended," said one, "choosing a wide array of outfits – from sporty shifts with sequined cocktail dresses, with sport coats and dark suits for the men."

Buried on a back page of this same edition of the *Times* was a story with the headline *Near-Riot Cuts Short Teen Program*:

CLEARWATER - A group of screaming teenagers climbed out of the bleachers at Jack Russell Stadium last night and tried to rush the bandstand where the Rolling Stones were belting out rock and roll music.

On the very same night St. Petersburg was formally dressed and applauding – for the first time in its history - Hollywood show business on a local stage, music history was being made in a ratty Clearwater baseball stadium. The two events could not have been more different – nor, as the *Times*' choice of coverage made clear, did anyone recognize the significance of the "near-riot." Teens, of course, were just teens, and the choices they made were fickle and unimportant.

The Stones' performance had been cut short that night, the band members directed to a waiting station wagon and hustled back to their hotel. They never finished the concert. "There will never be another show like this as long as I am here," the head of Clearwater's recreation department was quoted as declaring.

Afterwards, in his room at the Fort Harrison Hotel, Keith Richards came up with the music for "(I Can't Get No) Satisfaction." Mick Jagger wrote the lyrics the next day, at the pool.

"Satisfaction," of course, became the Rolling Stones' breakout record in America, in the summer of 1965, and one of the pillars of mid '60s rock 'n' roll. After "Satisfaction," many, many things would never again be the same.

And so the grand opening of the Bayfront Center was headline news, but not a watershed moment in popular culture – no, that was happening up the road in Clearwater.

GAY BLADES ROLLER RINK

October 18, 1965: Students from Shore Acres Elementary at Gay Blades Roller Rink. Zuma Press/Tampa Bay Times.

"All skate, all skate!"

When Elynor Gould's voice came over the public address system at Gay Blades Roller Rink, the skaters on the floor – sometimes numbering in the hundreds – knew that the couples' skate, backwards skate, Hokey Pokey or other specialty spotlight was over. "All skate" was the announcement that everyone, no matter their skill level, was allowed back onto the floor. It was time to roll.

Gay Blades was one of St. Petersburg's most popular recreation centers for nearly 35 years. The odd-looking building at 2191 9th Avenue North, with the Quonset Hut-style tin roof bolted to thin concrete walls, was home to the largest hardwood maple floor (90 by 180 feet) in the bay area.

Other roller skating rinks came and went in St. Pete – the Boulevard, the Pastime, the Pinellas, the Zink and Southland among them – but none had the staying power of Gay Blades, which opened in 1950 and was still packing 'em in when it was sold to make way for a medical arts building in 1985.

At least three generations of St. Petersburgers gracefully glided, stop-started hugging the railing, or fell repeatedly on that smooth and unyielding surface, bruising knees, elbows and derrieres.

With the exception of its first three years, the building was owned and operated by the Gould family, late of Des Moines, Iowa. Robert Gould and his wife Elynor ran a rink there, and when they moved to St. Pete, along with their three kids they brought several hundred pairs of rental skates, snack bar appliances and an old Hammond organ to provide music to skate to (the organist came along, too).

The St. Pete rink had been named in honor of the famous Gay Blades Rollerdrome, at 52nd Street and Broadway in New York. The Goulds leased and subsequently purchased the facility from the owner, who hadn't made much of a success of it.

Pre-World War II, roller skating was the province of adults almost exclusively. Bob Gould, who would become president of the RSROA (Roller Skating Rinks of America), was instrumental in getting younger and younger children into skates and onto the hardwood.

With the widespread scourge of juvenile delinquency becoming an

Mary Morrison, 14, competed in Junior Girls Freestyle. Morrison family photo.

The regional skating championships were often held at Gay Blades in the '50s and '60s. Bob Gould served as president of the RSROA (Roller Skating Rinks of America).

even greater problem, we have noticed many commendations in the daily newspapers, with regard to the wonderful aid being given to small communities by roller skating rinks. There are, according to juvenile authorities, far too few "supervised" recreational outfits for the youngsters, teen-agers and young adults, and it is only with "supervised" recreation that we are going to be able to attain the eventual reduction in such delinquency.

Gay Blades Newsletter (Roll Call), reprinted from Skating News, October 1954

"My dad hired a public relations man, George Russell, and he's the one who really got the youth coming there," remembers Frank "Buddy" Gould, 79. "He went around to the elementary schools and the junior high schools, and proposed that they sell tickets right there at the schools. Not at the rink. My mom used to stay up nights stamping the names of different schools on these tickets. And Dad would deliver them to the schools.

"And the schools could announce over the intercom that they were going to have a skating party. They sold the tickets for a dollar, and the school got 40 or 50 cents. So it was a fundraising thing for the school."

It was an ingenious marketing plan. Along with a percentage of ticket sales, the Goulds kept the snack bar profits, and the money from skate rentals.

"The ticket got you in the door, but if you didn't have your own skates, you had to rent them," says Buddy Gould, who was a competitive speed skater in his teens.

After-school "skating parties," with specially-chartered buses, took place weekdays (with separate hours for elementary and junior high kids). High schoolers and adults tended to come for the evening sessions, and the biggest crowds of all skated on Friday and Saturday nights.

Until a major renovation in 1976, the building was not air-conditioned. An aggregate of loud exhaust fans drew air through the translucent jalousie windows.

It was all part of the Gay Blades charm, according to Camilla Mosley, 68. "When you were born and raised here, the heat didn't bother you," she says.

Her family caught the Gay Blades bug in 1954. "My daddy skated, and so he taught all four of us kids to skate," she remembers. "And we all took lessons there; we were known as the Skating Mosleys; each one of us did something different.

"Everybody knew us at the skating rink. I skated in Southeastern Regionals and freestyle. I got the bronze medal. And my sister Debbie and her husband ended up in Nationals in 1984, and they came in fifth in the nation." She keeps photos from every era on her wall.

Young Camilla Mosley took private lessons during the week, learning to jump and spin. Other students were taught dance routines and performed in snappy costumes; still others aspired to be speed skaters.

Handsome Link Lester was a competitive skater, and an instructor.

Remembers his daughter, Tammy Lester Ingram: "They had a show in the late '50s, before I was born. For a charity. They put a slide up in the ceiling that they came out of, he said, going faster than lightning. He would come off the slide doing a freestyle jump."

Tammy took dance lessons at Gay Blades – but her father's legend loomed large. Everybody knew and admired Link Lester. "I was jealous because he was so, so good and I just didn't get that 'great' gene that he had," she laughs. "But I held my own."

She was at Gay Blades after school most days, and on the weekends. And she worked in the snack bar as a teen, in the '70s. "The skating rink was my whole life, basically," Tammy, 59, recalls. "Elynor was like a second grandmother to me. They were just wonderful people."

She met her husband, Jim Ingram, at the rink. He was a speed skater and a "floor guard" – a whistle-carrying referee, to put a stop to fights (which were infrequent) and generally keep the round-and-round flowing smoothly.

On the Facebook group page People Who Have Fond Memories of Gay Blades Roller Rink, certain themes are recurrent: My husband and I met there, I spent every weekend there, I learned to skate there, I competed in the Southeastern Regionals there, I broke my arm there, I always went after school, I won a pair of skates in Mr. Gould's raffle …

Friday nights were particularly important if you attended St. Petersburg High School, which was just three blocks west up 9th Avenue.

"We would all race to see who

December 13, 1966: Glenoak Elementary students at a Gay Blades afternoon skating party. Zuma Press/Tampa Bay Times.

would get down to the skating rink first to tell Mrs. Gould the score of the football game so she could announce it to the rink," Mosley, class of '69, recalls.

"I only got down there twice that I can remember, but I ran my butt off 'cause I didn't have a car. I ran as fast as I could and told Mrs. Gould the score. She would announce your name because you were the one who informed her. And it was a big deal to have your name announced over the intercom."

"We're very strict and believe in close supervision," says Mrs. Gould, the attractive, grey-haired matriarch of the rink, who personally supervises the whole show with an iron hand. A guard walks into the front office, and she chides him for a messy shirttail hanging out. "Are you going to tuck that in?" she challenges him. "No," he teases, but a moment later the guard skates by, shirttail neatly tucked in.

On Friday and Saturday nights the scene changes. The crowd is mostly teenagers looking for more than a couple hours frittered away on roller skates. A half hour before Gay Blades opens, the parking lot is almost empty, but already teens hang over the entrance rail, or sit on the roofs of cars, yelling greetings when someone new arrives.

Carolyn Nolte-Watts, St. Petersburg Times, June 17, 1974

In the mid 1970s, the one and a half-inch thick floor was ruined when the retention pond out back flooded during a thunderstorm. Bob Gould took out a small business loan to have the floor replaced and make additional upgrades.

Buddy Gould bought the business from his parents in 1976; he added a drop ceiling, better lights and a more powerful sound system for the house record player. And he changed the name to Gould's Roller Skating Rink.

His father died the following year. "A tireless worker, Mr. Gould devoted himself to the promotion of roller skating," read his obituary in the *St. Petersburg Times*.

During the "roller disco" craze of the late '70s, Buddy built a DJ booth and hired young record-spinners to broadcast the latest hits on weekends. "The DJ could manage the crowd with the music," he remembers, "and of course some of the kids brought their own records they wanted him to play."

Over time, the weekend nights began to attract different crowds. While white teenagers came to skate on Fridays, Saturdays became predominantly Black. It was, Gould explains, just a natural process. Something that organically happened.

Weekend evening skating hours were 8 to 11 p.m. both days. Saturday nights at 9:45, at his patrons' request, the skates came off and it turned into a dance party on the hardwood floor. These became known as "Soul Music Nights."

In June 1985, Gould agreed to sell Gay Blades lock, stock and skate rentals to Hospital Corporation of America, which owned the Edward H. White Hospital next door. The rink wasn't for sale – but, he explains, they made him an offer he couldn't refuse. The money was simply too good.

With a zoning change and other legalities on the table, half a year went by before HCA was able to take ownership and demolish the 35-year-old building. This gave Buddy Gould the time to wind down the school parties and the skating classes, and to arrange to donate the rental skates, video games and snack bar equipment to local charities.

"It'll do my heart good if they can get some use out of them," he told the newspaper that November. "I think I'll loaf for a few months."

The delay also provided those multiple generations of St. Petersburg skaters time to remember, and to grieve a time gone by.

"I took pictures during demolition," says Tammy Lester Ingram. "I stood there and I took pictures and I cried."

Gay Blades Roller Rink, photographed in 1964. Zuma Press/Tampa Bay Times.

DR. PAUL BEARER

Disc jockey and advertising man Dick Bennick created Dr. Paul Bearer in 1968, in High Point, North Carolina. WTOG promotional photo.

More than two decades after Dr. Paul Bearer left us for that great tenement castle in the sky, his legend lives on.

He still holds the record for the longest-ever continuous run as a TV horror-movie host, 22 years on WTOG's *Creature Feature*, which originated in St. Petersburg and was broadcast statewide. Several generations spent their Saturday afternoons in his company.

Dr. Paul Bearer's curious but good-natured blend of gallows humor and groan-inducing puns still hangs in the air, along with his cadaverous smile, enormous facial scar, disproportionate eyeballs and undertaker's costume.

And a voice like gravel and grease in a blender, chuckling diabolically while he discussed that day's "horrible old movie."

And an unforgettable singsong-y catchphrase: "I'll be luuuurking for you."

"A pun was the highest form of humor to him," says Patty Bennick, who was married to the man for the last nine years of his life. "And if I laughed at it, he knew it was funny. Because I hate puns."

Dr. Paul Bearer was Ernest Richard "Dick" Bennick, former stage magician, North Carolina "boss jock" and teenage dance-party host and, in his later years, regional sales manager for a pair of Lakeland radio stations.

He created Dr. Paul Bearer while working at WGHP in High Point, N.C. Dr. Bearer replaced Count Shockula, the station's first horror host, whom nobody (particularly Bennick, who wore the Shockula costume) liked very much.

"I realized that one of the reasons that the other character didn't work was the fact that he was not human," Bennick told blogger Ed Tucker in a 1991 interview. "You had no reason to empathize with him. When I changed characters, I had the same sets, the same props, the same coffin and the same jokes but it started to work. I think the reason is because Dr. Paul Bearer became a real person unto himself."

Finding the "look" took some thought, Bennick said. "I went through all these magazines and I picked out what I liked about various characters to design my new character. The beard came from a Vincent Price movie, and quite frankly I can't remember which one. Parting my hair down the middle I stole from a guy in New York, (TV/radio horror host) John Zacherley. The spats and the frock coat I just thought looked cool. I had to go to a beauty shop and get them to give me hair off the floor that matched my own to make the beard, because in those days they wouldn't let me grow one."

The scar was his pièce de résistance. "I could never explain the scar, I just kind of liked it and that seemed to make it click," he said.

"As the character continued to develop, I came up with two answers for where the scar came from. If a little kid asks me about it, I'd say I got it in a used scar lot! If it's an adult, I tell them I got it in the war and try to prompt them into saying well which war? I reply the boudoir (boo-d-war)!"

When Bennick moved to Polk County, Florida in 1973, Dr. Paul Bearer came with him. He convinced the WTOG station manager to give him a shot – and 22 years and thousands of horrible old movies later, he was as much of a St. Pete institution as Webb's City, Tropicana Field or even – yes, kids, it's true – Tyrone Square Mall.

"Dr. Paul Bearer's world is very real to him," Bennick said in that 1991 interview. "It's everyone else who is out of step, and when you stop and think about it, isn't that how most of us really are?"

They were a team, Dick and Patty. At home in Winter Haven, he meticulously wrote out all his gags, and prepared his props. They'd drive to the WTOG studio on Gandy Boulevard in St. Pete and, on a single Saturday, tape three months' worth of intros, outros and promos. She was the floor manager, in charge during the shoots on the purposely cheesy-looking tenement castle set.

"Let's face it, it's not a class act that I do," Dick admitted. "It's pretty schlocky when you get right down to it!

"There are a few things, though, that we try to pay attention to. One of those is don't pop the gag before I say it. That is a principle going back to the old burlesque blackout routines. That's what we try to do with the products. If I'm reading a Bleeder's Digest, don't show the magazine before I say Bleeder's Digest."

Her husband, Patty says, enjoyed all the attention, in and out of costume.

Dick had a prosthetic left eye – the result of a car accident years earlier – and because he also suffered from Grave's Disease (a pun he surely must have loved), his right eye had a pronounced bulge.

"We were checking into a hotel in Tampa, for an advertisers' convention," his wife recalls. "The girl at the front desk said 'Are you Dr. Paul Bearer?' and Dick said yes.

"She said 'I thought you had a glass eye?'

"He said 'I do!' And he pulled it out and showed it to her."

Patty Bennick cackles loudly at the memory. Just talking about her husband makes her laugh.

"One time I heard the guys on Q-105 talking about him," she says. "And they called him "Ol' Blue Eye.'"

Annoyed, she told her husband about it.

Hey, Bennick said, as long as they're talking about me, I don't care.

He made frequent public appearances, arriving in his decked out 1961 hearse, tossing out puns and signing autographs. "To a horribly good friend," he'd write, or "Horribly yours," or something equally corny.

Children adored him. Seniors, says Patty, seemed to be big fans, too (they never could figure that one out).

In 1993, Tampa mayor Sandra Freedman issued a proclamation designating Oct. 30 "Dr. Paul Bearer Day" in the city.

"I was thinking about running in politics myself when this is all over," Dr. Bearer said at the ceremony. "I'd champion all the dead issues. Of course, I'd have to be a fright-in candidate."

During parades, Patty would drive the hearse (slowly), while Dr. Bearer sat on the hood and spoke to his fans with a microphone. If a pedestrian strayed into the vehicle's path, he'd warn them: "Walk in front ... ride in back," and follow up with that ominous chuckle.

It wasn't always fun and games, however. "He was the Grand Marshal

"I came up with two answers for where the scar came from," Bennick said. "If a little kid asks me about it, I say I got it in a used scar lot! If it's an adult, I tell them I got it in the war and try to prompt them into saying well which war? I reply the boudoir (bood-war)!" WTOG promotional photo.

of a parade down in Lake Wales," remembers Patty. "And this church bus pulls up alongside of us, and they're all telling us that we're going to hell and all this kind of stuff. It had its ups and downs, for sure.

"In the Gasparilla Parade, in the float in front of us was a bunch of guys drinking. You know, it's the upper echelon of the Tampa/St. Pete area. I had my window down, because it was hot, and this guy comes over and said 'Here, can you take this beer can?' He wanted me to put it in the hearse, as his trash. I said no, and so he threw it at me.

"Dick had me stop the hearse. We got out of the parade line and left."

Then there was this: "When we were in the malls, signing autographs, he'd always sit with his back to the wall. Because one time somebody came up behind him and tried to hit him over the head with a 2x4. Because there were people who didn't like what the character represented."

Those were the exceptions, she insists. "Everybody loved him. They still do. I get calls from people all the time. I got a fan letter from a kid, he just wanted to have something of Dr. Paul Bearer's in the worst way. So I sent him a picture."

Dick Bennick died during heart bypass surgery on Feb. 20, 1995. He was 66.

"Someone once said that you are the sum of all your yesteryears, that is what makes you what you are today," he observed in 1991. "I brought together the fact that I have always had a hobby of magic, I have always loved puns, I always liked to dress up, I've always liked horror movies, and I enjoyed acting.

"You bring all this into play, and this is what comes out in Dr. Paul Bearer."

THE MOB

SUN HAVEN STUDIOS

When the Great Depression enveloped America in the late 1920s, the curtain had just come down on the silent film era. Spirit-lifting "talkies" were all the rage, when Pinellas County – and, in particular, the scrubby landscape of Weedon Island – came tantalizingly close to becoming the Hollywood of Florida.

Local developer Fred Blair's San Remo nightclub, shuttered by Prohibition, was idle and rotting away in early 1933. Smooth-talking Baltimore entreprenuer T.C. Parker arrived and convinced Blair to back him in a Florida movie studio; with the addition of Hollywood producer Aubrey Kennedy (to add authenticity to their project and act as a "lure" for others in the business), they purchased an additional 500 acres on Weedon Island.

The San Remo was to be gutted and refurbished as soundstages and office space for the ambitious project, initially called Kennedy City. Con-

A colorized lobby card for Playthings of Desire, the second of three films made on Weedon Island in 1933.

tracts, it was reported, were signed for 36 motion pictures.

Production began on *Chloe,* the first venture, on May 22, 1933. A drama set in the Louisiana bayou, it's the story of a young, white girl (silent film veteran Olive Borden) who's been raised in a shack by an old Black woman (Mandy, played by Georgette Harvey) she's always believed to be her mother.

Harvey's character happens to be a "voodoo priestess," and when doe-eyed young Chloe's birth family comes a-looking for her, there's hell to pay. Mandy vows revenge.

Putting aside the regrettable racial stereotypes of the era, the wooden acting (Borden never adapted to sound movies, and this would be her final performance) and the inane dialogue, *Chloe* (later re-titled *Chloe, Love is Calling You*) gives us fascinating, if brief, glimpses of 1933 Pinellas County:

The setting for numerous scenes (including the inevitable "love clinch" between Borden's Chloe and her beau-to-be, played by future B-movie star Reed Howes) looks very much like Lake Maggiore – then called Salt Lake – and the winding, wooden trails of what's now known as Boyd Hill Nature Park.

An alligator-wrestling scene that starts at water's edge (most likely a murky Weedon lagoon) continues with an underwater sequence shot 100 miles away at Silver Springs, where the water is crystal clear. And it's obvious the animal being "wrestled" is either drugged or already dead.

Other scenes were shot in the lush back yard of 630 20th Ave. Northeast, and at 305 South Hyde Park Avenue, Tampa.

The explosive finale, a (laughingly bad) nighttime "voodoo ceremony," features a dozen local extras, mostly African Americans, dancing around a bonfire at the base of a giant live oak tree draped in Spanish moss.

Kennedy told the *St. Petersburg Times* that work on *Chloe* would be completed on June 1. But several scenes had to be re-shot after an Eastern Air transport plane carrying reels of unprocessed film crashed near Bowling Green, Virginia on June 4.

The cast and crew toughed out the reshoots in the intense heat and

In Chloe: Georgette Harvey and St. Pete extras in full Louisiana "voodoo" mode.

bugs of early summer.

Kennedy and his in-house director Marshall Neilen made the front page of the *Evening Independent* May 23 with the announcement that silent film comedian Buster Keaton – "as a draw, second only to Chaplin" – was arriving in St. Petersburg to begin a five-year contract with the Weedon Island studio.

Keaton was having difficulty transitioning into "talkies," and the nascent studio system – where the big bosses, the money men, dictated every rule of production – was driving him to distraction.

(It later came to light that the deadpan star's alcoholism had actually caused his dismissal from a lucrative MGM contract.)

Kennedy and his backers promised him complete creative control, so

Keaton signed on the dotted line and flew to Florida.

Production on the first Keaton film is to start here in about three weeks. The new sound stage will be completed by that time and will be ready for use ... with the coming to St. Petersburg of Keaton, St. Petersburg becomes second only to Hollywood in importance in the moving picture business.

Evening Independent/May 23, 1933

On July 2, the *Times* reported that Keaton and director Neilen had traveled to Havana, Cuba to scout additional locations for *The Fisherman,* the comedian's first Kennedy-made feature. The film, it was revealed, was to begin shooting "within the week" on Weedon Island.

Keaton leased an 11-room house on Snell Island, moved his wife and brother in, and was awarded the key to the city during a celebration at Williams Park. He played baseball for the Coca-Cola Bottlers, a St. Petersburg amateur team.

"The comedian kept the grounds in an uproar with his nonchalance at third base and his antics at the plate," reported the *Independent*, "swinging six or seven bats and calling the balls and strikes for the umpire."

As work progressed on *The Fisherman,* however, the silent film legend grew discouraged with the area – particularly the humidity, which melted his heavy makeup and attracted insects, which stuck to his face. And with the Kennedy complex, which he complained was unfinished and lacked the technical personnel he required.

Silent film star Buster Keaton planned to make several movies in St. Petersburg.

After less than three months in St. Petersburg, Keaton got on a plane and never returned; *The Fisherman* was left incomplete.

"As far as I knew he never got before a camera," *Evening Independent* editor William G. Wiley would later write. "He did most of his work in a local bar where, from time to time, he entertained the customers by taking off his pants and sweeping the floor with them."

Work began just after Independence Day on Kennedy's second picture. Directed by George Melford, *Playthings of Desire* was a melodrama about wealthy New Yorker Jim Malvern (James Kirkwood) who brings his new bride Gloria Dawn (Linda Watkins) from her New York home to his vast estate in Florida. There, a fun-loving "gang" of his city friends arrives as a surprise.

Things don't go well, as the partiers quickly begin to wear out their welcome, and Malvern renews his acquaintance with old flame Anne (Josephene Dunn).

Reed Howes, the he-man hero of *Chloe*, returns as the he-man hero who saves Gloria from both humiliation and, in the end, a murder charge. Molly O'Day, who'd had a small role in *Chloe*, is also in the cast.

The first scene committed to film, on July 5, 1933, may be the best part of *Playthings of Desire*. The entire cast frolics in the Bayou Farms public swimming pool, at 5150 4th Street South, with Little Bayou and Tampa Bay clearly visible in the background.

There's also a short sequence with the original Gandy Bridge over the actors' shoulders.

Other scenes were shot in the wilds of Weedon, including one where a scary alligator - clearly tethered to the ground – attempts to "get at" Gloria (who faints dead away at the very sight of it).

The sprawling Donald Roebling Estate, in the Harbor Oaks area of Clearwater, stood in for Malvern's oceanside mansion.

Playthings of Desire (U.K. title: *Mur-*

der in the Library) had its world premiere in September at the Capitol Theatre in St. Petersburg, with hundreds of locals in attendance.

Even the ever-cheerleading Times had trouble saying anything positive about the film. "While the plot is thin, it nevertheless is interesting," read the next day's review.

The writer instead praised the scenery. "Much of the beauty of the settings for the picture is due entirely to nature, for nothing artificial had to be added to make the scenes more effective."

Just as production was getting underway on Hired Wife, the studio's third picture, Parker and a group of New York financiers bought out Kennedy's interest in the company. A new production entity, Sun Haven Studios, would assume control and distribute the films.

"We plan to produce feature and program pictures at reasonably moderate costs," Parker told the Times. "Nothing gigantic like Gold Diggers or 42nd Street, but the best pictures possible for $50,000. Some may run as low as $20,000."

Parker also boasted that his company's deal with the long-gone Keaton, for The Fisherman and other titles, was still in place, despite the fact that the comedian had already dissolved his prospective St. Pete production company, Flamingo Films, Inc. and returned to California.

Starring heavily-accented Norwegian silent film actress Greta Nissen, Hired Wife (U.K. title: Marriage of Convenience) began production in September on Weedon Island, with other scenes created at the Soreno Hotel in downtown St. Petersburg, and at the Florida Theater on 5th Street South. Returning director George Melford also shot a lengthy scene on and around the Eastern Air landing strip and airport facility on Weedon.

The cast included Kirkwood (from

> **In 1934, federal agents swooped in and closed Parker's movie complex for failure to pay taxes, taking the master prints of "Chloe," "Playthings of Desire" and "Hired Wife" with them.**

DVD covers for Chloe and Playthings of Desire; Greta Nissen in Hired Wife.

Playthings) and, in her third St. Pete film, Molly O'Day.

By the time *Hired Wife* premiered in March, 1934, Sun Haven Studios was a memory. According to the Internet Movie Database, federal agents swooped in and closed Parker's movie complex for failure to pay taxes, taking the master prints of *Chloe*, *Playthings of Desire* and *Hired Wife* with them.

Weedon Island's final filmmaking foray is not to be confused with *Hired Wife*, the 1940 screwball comedy starring Rosalind Russell.

Never restored, *Chloe* and *Playthings of Desire* are viewable online and as blurry DVD transfers; although prints of *Hired Wife* are known to exist, it is currently unavailable.

Today, no evidence of the film buildings remain on Weedon Island; the story of Aubrey Kennedy, Buster Keaton and Sun Haven Studios gets but a passing mention in the history section of the Weedon Island State Preserve Visitors' Center.

H.E.A.L.T.H.

Director Robert Altman and an all-star cast made H.E.A.L.T.H. at the Don CeSar Resort on St. Petersburg Beach in 1979. The incomprehensible dark comedy never went into general release; President Ronal Reagan had it privately screened and proclaimed it "The world's worst movie." All photos: 20th Century Fox.

When filmmaker Robert Altman and a cast of A-list stars set up camp at the Don Ce Sar Resort in 1979, everyone went - briefly - berserk. It's always exciting when Hollywood comes to Anytown, USA to make a movie, and the community, along with the media, rolled out the red carpet for Altman, Lauren Bacall, Carol Burnett, James Garner, Glenda Jackson, Dick Cavett and an enormous crew.

Writing in the *St. Petersburg Times*, Roy Peter Clark called their arrival "The biggest thing to happen in St. Pete Beach since the Great Hurricane of 1921" and, after watching a few minutes of daily footage, predicted that *Health*, as Altman's dark comedy was to be called, "will rank with *M*A*S*H* and *Nashville* among Altman's greatest films."

Forty years later, almost nobody has seen *Health* (also known as *H.E.A.L.T.H.*) After a disastrous debut in California theaters, 20th Century Fox - which spent nearly $6 million making the movie – shelved it. It appeared, briefly, at film festivals and on TV in the early 1980s.

President Ronald Reagan arranged a private screening at Camp David, and pronounced it "The world's worst movie."

To date, *Health* has never been made available in any home video format.

In recent years, high-profile titles including *The Infiltrator, Magic Mike* and the *Dolphin Tale* films were lensed, at least partially, in Pinellas County. And longtime residents still talk fondly of a mid '80s hot streak that included Ron Howard's *Cocoon*, and the John Candy comedy *Summer Rental*.

But *Health*?

Like *Nashville, A Wedding* and others in the Altman oeuvre, *Health* is a sprawling film that features an ensemble of main characters, overlapping storylines and a central plot that meanders through sight gags, romances, red herrings and the often ridiculous.

Cavett, playing himself, is shooting an episode of his chat show at a beachside convention of health-food suppliers, business-people and assorted kooks. The governing organization, HealtH ("Happiness, Energy and Longevity Through Health") is electing a new president – the candidates are a narcoleptic octogenarian (Bacall) and a bloviating

Clockwise from left: Burnett, Bacall, Jackson and Altman. Despite such star power, the movie was a disaster.

windbag (Jackson), neither of whom makes a strong case one way or the other.

Altman said later that the film, which would have come out during the 1980 presidential election, was a political satire. Bacall's Esther Brill was supposed to represent Dwight D. Eisenhower, while Jackson's Isabella Garnell was Adlai Stevenson (indeed, sections of Jackson's tiresome speeches were lifted from Stevenson's real-life pronouncements). Its intention was to lampoon politics, commercialism and the media.

Are we laughing yet?

The main characters (at least those with the most screen time) are Burnett, as "White House health specialist" Gloria Burbank, and James Garner as Harry Wolff, her ex-husband, who just happens to be there as an assistant to Bacall's eccentric character.

This should have ensured something surefire. Garner's The Rockford Files was one of the hottest shows on TV in 1979, and Burnett's much-loved variety show had only recently gone off the air.

The company arrived in March. Health, it was announced, had a budget of $5.6 million and was scheduled for a seven-week shoot, all of it at the Don Ce Sar. During a press conference at the hotel, Burnett – who had previously starred with Health screenwriter and cast member Paul Dooley in Altman's A Wedding – was quick to bring up the Equal Rights Amendment, which had not yet been ratified by the Florida legislature.

"I'm down here primarily for the ERA. I couldn't care less about Mr. Altman," the ebullient actress exclaimed, to a round of laughs from the local media.

"I wanted to come because I want to work with Bob any time that I can, and it's fitting in beautifully because this is an important time for Florida. I'll do whatever I can."

Media reports noted that Jackson,

James Garner and Lauren Bacall at the Don CeSar.

the Academy Award-winning British actress, looked "uncomfortable" during the press event, and barely spoke a word.

Clark, who teaches writing at the Poynter Institute, remembers those star-studded days well. "Because the venue was the Don, you couldn't block it off," he says. "And so it was a very, very public shooting. There were a lot of people around. I walked around the Don – and even though I was covering, I don't remember even having to show a credential."

He remembers passing screen legend Bacall, wearing an "old lady smock," her hair in curlers, in an upstairs hallway.

Altman's production company had taken over the entire hotel; interior scenes for *Health* were shot in various suites and convention rooms.

Because he wrote extensively about the production in the *Times*, Clark was given access to Altman – and, over time, to the above-the-title stars – for exclusive interviews.

Despite his perceived status as a cheerleader, Clark says now, he saw warning signs that *Health* was maybe, possibly not going to pull through.

At Altman's invitation, he sat in on a screening of the auteur's most recent films, including the futuristic *Quintet*, starring Paul Newman.

"It's when I saw these other movies that I realized something not-so-good was going on," Clark says. *Quintet*, he realized, "was derivative. It was really, really weak Bergmann."

It dawned on Clark, at that moment, that Altman was spreading his talents too thin by making *too many* movies in a row. *Health* was his 15th feature in as many years. What was the rush?

"My terrible prediction about *Health*, in 1979, came from the cast – how could something with Glenda Jackson, Carol Burnett, James Garner, Lauren Bacall, Henry Gibson and Dick Cavett go wrong? And with one of the great American filmmakers?"

How, indeed? At this writing, the full movie is available on YouTube, and Altman scholars agree it represents the filmmaker at the nadir of his gift – it's long, and it's talky and it is supremely unfunny.

Interestingly, except for a few long shots of the unmistakable pink exterior and rooftop minarets, very little in the film can be identified as the Don Ce Sar. *Health* could have been shot in any big hotel – you don't even see much of the beach – in any other Anytown, USA.

After a brief public dust-up with the local Teamsters about transportation costs ("They make their own contracts – it's blackmail"), Altman finished *Health* two weeks ahead of schedule, declaring on the last day of filming that the shoot, and the St. Pete community, was "superb on every level. I wouldn't have one single complaint."

It was reported that $2 million had been pumped into the local economy.

During his squabble with the union, Altman met with Florida governor Bob Graham. Among other things, they discussed the possibility that the director would make his next film, *Popeye* (with Robin Williams), in the state.

Production on *Popeye*, in the end,

Lauren Bacall and Dick Cavett in the movie's opening scene, behind the hotel.

went to Malta, and Altman never returned to Florida. It would be a dozen years before his career would go on the upswing again, with *The Player, Short Cuts, Gosford Park* and *Pret-a-Porter*. He died in 2006.

Viewed as a time capsule of St. Petersburg Beach in the 1970s – hundreds of local folks appear as extras in the movie's many convention scenes – *Health* does have some redemptive value.

And Roy Peter Clark got something substantial out of the experience.

"Our youngest daughter, Lauren, was born in 1980," the writer explains. "She had been Renee for quite some time in our planning, my wife and I, until I got to interview Lauren Bacall. She was fantastic. I think I was overwhelmed by her glamor."

COCOON

From left: Brimley, Cronyn and Ameche in the "Fountain of Youth," on Park Street in St. Petersburg. 20th Century Fox

Because of its popularity as a retirement destination, and the subsequent preponderance of an elderly population, sleepy St. Petersburg had a nickname: God's Waiting Room.

Although the unfortunate tag is usually attributed to Johnny Carson, no one really knows where it came from.

Of course, nobody calls it that any more, as St. Petersburg has evolved into a center for business, bohemia and the arts.

But it was that God's Waiting Room thing that drew 20th Century Fox Location Manager Bob Maharis to the city in 1984, to scout places to shoot the $17.5 million fantasy film *Cocoon* – in which three feisty old-timers discover a group of benevolent aliens who happen to hold the secret to immortality.

"It will photograph well," Maharis told a *St. Petersburg Times* reporter on the first day of shooting, Aug. 20, in Williams Park. "It has a nice feel. We felt the old people here were more energetic. They ride bicycles, they go to the Coliseum to dance."

Cocoon's director was 30-year-old Ron Howard, four years out of *Happy Days* and fresh off box office gold with his third directorial effort, *Splash*.

In a 20th Century Fox "making-of" featurette, Howard, sitting on one of the Boca Ciega Bay sets, looks – and sounds – just like TV's Richie Cunningham, his big-boy mustache notwithstanding. He was still many years from *Apollo 11*, *The Da Vinci* Code and his Academy Award for *A Beautiful Mind.*

> *Cast and crew descended on the city and worked for 12 weeks. The Coast Guard gave the company use of several airplane hangars to shoot interior scenes.*

"Often when you go into a town, it can be a little touch-and-go," he says. "Particularly after a little while, they start to feel like the movie company's running the town. That hasn't occurred here. It's been just the opposite. We've had nothing but cooperation."

The cast included veteran actors Don Ameche, Hume Cronyn, Jessica Tandy, Gwen Vernon, Maureen Stapleton and Jack Gilford. Wilford Brimley was the relative newcomer. He turned 50 during production; his brown hair and walrus mustache were dyed white to make him appear older.

Also in town for the duration were Brian Dennehy and Tahnee Welch (Raquel's daughter) as aliens-in-disguise, and Steve Guttenberg as the charter boat operator who stumbles upon their secret.

According to the story by David Saperstein (re-written for the film script by Tom Benedek), the space travelers – Antareans – have returned to earth to retrieve fallen comrades, who were left there thousands of years before, encased in protective cocoons in the depths of the Gulf of Mexico.

Dennehy, Welch and their crew hire Guttenberg's boat to retrieve the cocoons, and deliver them to a secret swimming pool they've charged with "life force." Suitably revived, the cocooned aliens will leave Earth when the mothership arrives to take everybody home.

Remember, this was just two years after Steven Spielberg's *E.T.* (Early on, Howard jokingly referred to the story as *Close Encounters on Golden Pond*.)

Unfortunately for the Antareans, the house-with-pool they've rented for the mission is next door to a retirement home. And oldsters Ameche, Cronyn and Brimley have a

habit of hopping the fence to take a refreshing swim now and again.

Suncoast Manor Retirement Community, the Pinellas Point facility filling in for the fictional retirees' "rest home," was miles away from the swimming pool, behind a Park Street mansion on Boca Ciega Bay. Such is the magic of Hollywood.

The filmmakers built a structure over and around the outdoor pool. This way, the trio of escapees from "Sunny Shores" could enjoy their swim away from prying eyes. And the Antareans's business – hauling the cocoons from Guttenberg's boat and sliding them into the pool – could go on in secret.

The trouble starts – the central plot is set in motion – when the old guys,

Howard (kneeling at center) and his cast in the Park Street "pool house." At bottom right are the film's producers, Lili and Richard Zanuck. 20th Century Fox.

swimming in the water with the cocoons and the "life force," begin to feel energized, rejuvenated. Turns out the juiced pool water has a way of making old humans "young again." It's what Ponce de Leon had been looking for - the Fountain of Youth.

That's essentially it. Although reviews were mixed (the ending both tugs on the heartstrings and stretches disbelief), *Cocoon* was the sixth highest grossing film of 1985. At 77, Don Ameche won an Oscar.

Cast and crew descended on the city and worked for 12 weeks. The Coast Guard gave the company use of several airplane hangars to shoot interior scenes. Except for several underwater shots (lensed afterwards in the Bahamas) and the Industrial Light and Magic sequences for the woo-woo ending, all of the film was lensed in St. Petersburg.

Looking at *Cocoon* now, it's a treasure trove of 1980s St. Pete, from the downtown shuffleboard courts to

Dennehy and Guttenberg aboard the Manta III, the working sportfishing vessel purchased for the shoot by Twentieth Century Fox. An exact replica of the boat was built out of plywood and fiberglass, with no keel or engines – nothing, in fact, below the waterline. This was done because the water behind the Park Street home, in 1984, was just 15 inches deep. The actual Manta III, therefore, could not be brought up to the "dock" for the "aliens" to unload the "cocoons. 20th Century Fox.

John's Pass, from the Snell Arcade to Northeast Shopping Center. The first scene captured on film, Aug. 20 at Williams Park, was a cutting-room-floor casualty.

A lengthy sequence was shot, in a single day, at the St. Petersburg Coliseum.

Cronyn, then 73, tried parasailing. Brimley caught a giant tarpon, fishing from the beach behind the St. Petersburg Hilton, where the cast was staying.

Vernon told the *Times* they all dined at Leverock's, Giovanni's and the Lobster Pot, and enjoyed the Don CeSar breakfast buffet.

Stapleton set up the board game Trivial Pursuit in the Hilton lobby and challenged all comers, sometimes playing until the wee hours.

Sundays were days off. They dropped by the Dali Museum (the first incarnation, on 3rd Street), Sunken Gardens and the soon-to-close London Wax Museum. Charter buses were organized for day trips to Busch Gardens.

Howard, his pregnant wife and their 3-year-old daughter, future film star Bryce Dallas Howard, visited Fort De Soto.

Only Guttenberg and Dennehy, two of the youngest cast members, apparently sampled the nightlife. Silas Dent's was a favorite. On Oct. 16, as the two were leaving Bennigan's on 66th Street, driver Dennehy made an illegal U-turn. The officer who pulled him over administered a sobriety test, which he failed, and the Canadian actor spent the night in jail.

"The cop was very nice," Dennehy told writer Steve Persall in 2010. "Poor Guttenberg was frantic about the whole thing ... I should've let Steve drive and I didn't because I'm dumb, Irish and willful."

Because the state film industry at the time, such as it was, did not keep precise records of expenditures, there's no dollar figure on the impact *Cocoon* made on the local economy during the 12 weeks of production in St. Pete. But it took in $85.3 million at the box office.

Thirty-six years after the events, only Guttenberg and Welch are still with us. And Ron Howard, of course.

In that "making-of" video from '84, he reveals one of the more pleasant surprises about working on *Cocoon*:

"All of our background people, with small parts and extras, we've been able to cast here in St. Petersburg – with a lot of people who haven't worked in pictures since the silent days!

"But it's great; I get up and talk to them about it, and say 'Gee, you're doing very well.' And they'll say 'Well, I know a little something about this. I was with D.W. Griffith in 1913.' Or 'I was making pictures in New Jersey as an extra, working as a kid, and I remember.'"

"I ask them if it's changed. And they say 'No, it hasn't changed too much.'"

Acknowledgements

Thanks to Rui Farias, Jessica Breckenridge and Nevin Sitler of the St. Petersburg Museum of History, to Amy Cianci, Joe Hamilton and Pablo Guidi of St. Petersburg Press, and to Darrell Horton, Jon Bortles, Benjamin Kirby, Curtis Graham and all the kind folks from the *Fond Memories of Gay Blades Roller Rink* Facebook group.

And thank you to the hardworking reporters from the *St. Petersburg Times* (aka *Tampa Bay Times*) and *Evening Independent*, whose daily documentation of St. Pete activities was crucial to much of the research that went into this book. If you hadn't been taking notes then, there would be nothing to talk about today.

For Amy, as always.

Other books by Bill DeYoung

Skyway: The True Story of Tampa Bay's Signature Bridge and the Man Who Brought it Down (University Press of Florida)

Phil Gernhard Record Man (University Press of Florida)

I Need to Know: The Lost Music Interviews (St. Petersburg Press)

Next Generation Local News.

Subscribe to the Daily Spark and get St. Pete's latest business and civic news in your inbox.

stpetecatalyst.com

Brought to you by

ST. PETERSBURG
PRESS

Author-centric publishing

stpetersburgpress.com